T0328890

Every day that our health care systems malfunction, there is a huge opportunity cost in terms of money, mortality, morbidity, on-going health disparities, and patient frustration. I believe that this book has a huge potential to solve many problems using less resources and less time.

Michael Kanter, MD., CPPS, Professor and Chair of Clinical Science;
Kaiser Permanente Bernard J. Tyson School of Medicine;
former Regional Medical Director of Quality & Clinical Analysis, Kaiser
Permanente

The American healthcare system is replete with paradoxes. The system has an abundance of resources, outstanding medical centers and extraordinarily well-trained doctors and other health care professionals. Yes, despite the high costs the results are inconsistent resulting from waste and inefficiency. In this book Professor Oppenheim outlines the Lean Healthcare Systems Engineering methodology which, properly implemented can reduce waste and create a more reliable healthcare system. With this methodology the future for American healthcare is bright. Brilliant!

Howard Fullman, MD, FACP, GACG, AGAF, Medical Director and
Chief of Staff Emeritus, Kaiser Permanente, West Los Angeles

The very complex and fragmented US healthcare system continues to challenge us to meet the needs of patients and providers for care that is affordable and of consistent high quality. Dr. Oppenheim's book on Lean Healthcare Systems Engineering (LHSE) offers a straightforward rigorously applied methodology that serves as a very effective approach toward achieving measurable and impactful improvements in the efficiency and quality of care. I can confidently recommend his book based on my personal experience as a physician leader who has successfully employed LHSE and its Lean enablers to improve healthcare delivery in a variety of clinical settings.

F. Ronald Feinstein, DMD, MD, FACS, Clinical Professor of
Surgery Keck School of Medicine of USC; Assistant Area
Medical Director and Physician Manager Surgical and
Support Services Emeritus Kaiser-WLA; Regional Chief of
Plastic Surgery Emeritus Southern California
Permanente Medical Group

The book and author's thoughtful and robust insights are the perfect prescription for anyone with a serious desire to remedy the complex, fragmented, and broken healthcare delivery system. The technical details and real-life examples provide a much needed road map for the journey from theory to actual and attainable, practical improvement.

Gail Lindsay, RN, MA, SCAL Region Chief Quality Officer,
Providence St. Joseph

Based on my own experience, both as a practicing Chief of Pediatrics and as an Assistant Area Medical Director responsible for Quality Improvement, this is a very readable, yet thorough work grounded in the reality of actually improving medical care. A groundbreaking contribution to the field. Masterful.

Stephen Tarzynski, MD., MPH, Kaiser Permanente, President of California Physicians Alliance (CaPA)

This book supplies a roadmap for anyone interested in taking the best aspects of systems engineering and lean thinking and applying them in a pragmatic way to healthcare delivery. It is understandable by everyone, but valuable even to experienced practitioners.

Christopher Unger, Ph.D., INCOSE Healthcare Working Group Leader Chief Systems Engineer, GE Healthcare

The application of systems engineering and lean processes to the healthcare industry is an important enabler to the INCOSE vision of "a better world through a systems approach." This text describes a new process Lean Healthcare Systems Engineering (LHSE) for managing workflow and care improvement projects in clinical environments. Following the step-by-step process identified in this text can contribute to higher quality of project work and project results with fewer frustrations, I encourage readers to give it a try!

Marilee J. Wheaton, President-Elect and Fellow, International Council for Systems Engineering (INCOSE), Systems Engineering Fellow, The Aerospace Corporation

More now than ever with the pandemic the Lean Healthcare System Engineering will expeditiously address systems issues, so this book is timely.

Jamie Gearon, Chief, Process Improvement Office, VA Greater Los Angeles Healthcare System

I train/coach individuals and teams who are embedded in healthcare provider organizations directly. I would recommend this book to my apprentices as a valuable complementary perspective from someone who has seen it, done it and is teaching it.

Dr. S. R. Dodds MA, MS, FRCS. Health Care Systems Engineer and Consultant Surgeon, United Kingdom

Lean Healthcare Systems Engineering for Clinical Environments

A Step-by-Step Process for Managing Workflow and Care Improvement Projects

Bohdan W. Oppenheim

Routledge
Taylor & Francis Group

NEW YORK AND LONDON

First published 2021
by Routledge
600 Broken Sound Parkway #300, Boca Raton FL, 33487

and by Routledge
2 Park Square, Milton Park, Abingdon, Oxon, OX14 4RN

Routledge is an imprint of the Taylor & Francis Group, an informa business

Library of Congress Cataloging-in-Publication Data
A catalog record has been requested for this book

ISBN: 978-0-367-75533-1 (hbk)
ISBN: 978-0-367-75532-4 (pbk)
ISBN: 978-1-003-16283-4 (ebk)

Typeset in Garamond
by MPS Limited, Dehradun

The author dedicates this book to the brave medical professionals who risked their lives saving COVID-19 patients during the 2020 pandemic. Many of them became infected, some gave their lives, others worked under unbelievable stress and discomfort in their PPEs, and many worked without proper PPEs because their government failed them...

Contents

List of Figures, Tables, and Numbered Text Boxes

Figures

Tables

Numbered Text Boxes

Foreword

It has been almost 20 years since the Institute of Medicine released the seminal report titled *Crossing the Quality Chasm*. They identified six domains of care quality (safe, timely, effective, efficient, equitable, and patient-centric) and noted a huge gap between the current state and the desired state. Although this report received a great deal of attention, sadly, there has been little progress in these areas. In the United States, healthcare still has huge disparities, is inefficient, and is fragmented with delays in care that are often unsafe. Most U.S. citizens are expected to suffer from a diagnostic error sometime during their lifetime, not receive a large fraction of recommended care, and pay for one of the most expensive systems in the world.

Much has been written about quality improvement over the years by many prominent quality and safety experts. Yet progress has been slow. Some have called on the healthcare professions to look outside of healthcare to other industries, using examples in nuclear power and airlines for safety, the hotel and entertainment industry for a "customer" focus, and the automotive industry, particularly Toyota for efficiency (Lean).

This book by Dr. Bohdan Oppenheim on lean healthcare systems engineering (LHSE) is a fresh approach that brings forth concepts that systems engineers have used in huge national defense projects. These massive projects involve many companies and people widely distributed in many locations who need to work together to solve complex coordination problems. What is unique in this book is that these powerful system engineering tools are modified to be able to address smaller sized healthcare problems that still involve similar problems in fragmentation and poor communication and coordination.

LHSE does use some techniques familiar to most practitioners of healthcare quality like fishbone diagrams, process mapping, and Lean. Often, in much quality work, however, these useful tools are deployed in isolation or perhaps with a PDSA cycle (plan, do, study, act). Yet these tools applied alone and in isolation may not always be powerful enough to address the needed quality improvement in healthcare. Instead, they offer a fragmented approach and result in a great deal of time-consuming and expensive trial and error. Oftentimes, the common trial and error approach creates a huge temptation to torture the outcomes data until it looks like a solution has been achieved. On the other hand, LHSE creates a very systematic and rigorous methodology that uses these and other popular tools but organizes them into a systematic approach to problem-solving.

Using a Lean philosophy of not creating an improvement system that is in itself wasteful, LHSE, as taught in this book, removes much of the waste and complexity of systems engineering used in large-scale engineering projects without removing their essential rigor needed in healthcare. It has been shown to work in a wide range of modest-sized projects involved in many different aspects of healthcare.

Typical systems of improvement used in healthcare like PDSA are useful, but they do not address the fundamental nature of the fragmentation in healthcare. Although widely used, such techniques have not lived up to their promise of creating a better healthcare system.

LHSE, although rigorous, does not require any engineering or mathematical expertise. It does, however, require some precision in thinking and reasoning.

Some other differences between LHSE and other approaches should be noted. In LHSE, great care is taken not to jump to a solution prematurely. Many traditional approaches to quality make an incorrect assumption that the problem is obvious and requires little thought to describe it.

Although it should be obvious, reviewing existing published literature is one of the first steps, but in my experience, this is not done or it is done poorly, thus leading to projects that are ill defined and often repeat mistakes of the past.

The background phase of LHSE emphasizes the review of any prior studies that address the situation of interest.

LHSE also emphasizes the need to list precise system requirements. The requirements that are stated in LHSE are often left off other healthcare improvement methodologies. Again, not systematically delineating requirements of a newly proposed system can lead to failure to address all of the important issues and result in inefficient trial and error. LHSE, by mandating that system requirements be clearly delineated, adds more rigor. In my experience, one of the main reasons a project may fail is that there are no requirements defined, and if there are, they are not achieved.

Not infrequently quality efforts not only assume the problem statement is trivial and easy to arrive at, but they also prematurely jump to a solution. LHSE, on the other hand, requires one to create an analysis of alternatives which is another novel approach not found in other healthcare improvement approaches. The classic PDSA cycle may just pick one solution and try it out, depending on how much planning goes into the planning portion of the cycle. In LHSE, one keeps several candidate solutions in mind and formally rates them prior to choosing an approach. This can avoid the oftentimes frustrating trial and error approach otherwise used.

Lastly, prior to implementation, LHSE requires an assessment of the risks involved as well as verification and validation of proposed solutions.

All of this rigor can be done without a huge amount of resources and has the potential to create system improvements that have been carefully and rigorously analyzed without paralysis by analysis. The advantage is that costly and time-consuming trial and error is minimized, and a more systematic approach is used. This book clearly and concisely presents the basic elements of LHSE.

Besides the LHSE process, the book contains 63 tabularized summaries of typical healthcare projects in clinics, hospitals, including OR and ED, laboratories, pharmacies, and ancillary departments. Called Lean Enablers because they are based on Lean thinking of reducing waste while promoting value, they list recommended major project steps. The enablers should facilitate many healthcare project improvements.

Every day that our health care systems malfunction, there is a huge opportunity cost in terms of money, mortality, morbidity, on-going health disparities, and patient frustration. I believe that this book has a huge potential to solve many problems using less resources and less time.

Michael Kanter, M.D., CPPS
Professor and Chair of Clinical Science,
Kaiser Permanente School of Medicine
Former Regional Medical Director of Quality & Clinical Analysis,
Kaiser Permanente

Preface

This book is written for two purposes:

1. To popularize and provide a reference text for a powerful new process called **Lean Healthcare Systems Engineering (LHSE)** for managing workflow and care improvement projects in all clinical environments. The book applies to ambulatory sites (called "clinics" throughout the book) and hospitals of all types, including operating rooms, emergency departments, ancillary departments, clinical and imaging laboratories, pharmacies, and population health activities. The book presents a generic step-by-step process of systems engineering, strongly tailored for healthcare workflows and guided by Lean thinking.
2. To serve as a reference text for the first major product created with the LHSE process, called Lean Enablers for Healthcare Projects. The enablers are tabularized comprehensive summaries of representative projects in healthcare delivery applications. Each enabler reduces waste and promotes value. Each enabler table includes project challenges, improvement ideas, and a summary of project steps. Hopefully, the enablers will make the practice of healthcare professionals easier than traditional approaches.

The aim of the book is to demonstrate that:

- **Healthcare projects critically need the systems engineering process.**
- **Systems engineering can bring extraordinary practical benefits to healthcare projects.**

■ **Most healthcare projects need only a simplified version of systems engineering, dramatically reduced in complexity relative to the traditional version used in large engineering programs. This text presents a version of the systems engineering process focused on healthcare and strongly simplified using the wisdom of Lean thinking. We named it Lean Healthcare Systems Engineering (LHSE) process.**

■ **No prior engineering background is needed to use the LHSE process.**

The term **Systems Engineering (SE)** is somewhat misleading as it conjures images of engineering and mathematical formulas. Not so. It is a historical term. The discipline of *Systems Engineering* (SE) was created by Si Ramo and Dean Woldridge in 1954 to help with the development of ballistic missiles, which had to work unconditionally [Jacobsen, 2001]. It is a heuristic body of knowledge more akin to project management but focused on managing flow of information in fragmented systems, while project management tends to focus on management of resources. The reader familiar with project management will recognize some overlap with the present material [Rebentisch, 2017]. Since healthcare is the largest fragmented system in human civilization, systems engineering finds a perfectly fertile ground in healthcare applications, rigorously integrating fragmented elements into robust care solutions. However, to make it useful in typical small healthcare projects, the classical systems engineering had to be strongly reduced in complexity from its version used in defense, aerospace, infrastructure, energy, and automotive programs. The author placed a big emphasis on making this simplified version of systems engineering "lean and user friendly" for healthcare professionals.

Lean [Womack and Jones, 1996] contributed the wisdom of maximizing value while minimizing waste, project effort, cost, and schedule. The Lean definition of waste is "anything other than what is absolutely required to deliver value to the [patient or healthcare] customer" [Oppenheim, 2011]. This definition was used to tailor the classical systems engineering process down to what this author believes is truly needed in typical healthcare projects. Applied as an integrated body of knowledge of healthcare, systems engineering, and Lean, **LHSE** is a process that contributes logical rigor, higher quality of both project work and project results, savings in project effort, cost, and schedule, and most importantly, better care, fewer frustrations, and less burnout to stakeholders.

We use classical Lean to reduce waste and streamline work processes. A twin body of knowledge of Six Sigma[1] [Harry and Shroeder, 2000] is used to elevate process bottlenecks and imperfections. Industrial experience indicates that both are needed. The integrated body of knowledge is often called Lean Six Sigma [Wedgewood, 2007]. In the present book, for brevity, we use the term "Lean" as meaning integrated **Lean Six Sigma**.

The book is a result of the author's seven years of experience as a faculty and the director of a unique Healthcare Systems Engineering graduate program at Loyola Marymount University[2] and, more importantly, academic advisor or co-advisor for 57 semester-long capstone projects, soon to be 100, conducted by master's students at Kaiser Permanente, UCLA Health, USC Keck/LA County hospitals, VA Los Angeles, Cedar Sinai, Providence St. Joseph and AltaMed. Prior to this activity, for almost 20 years, the author served in a number of leadership positions in various national bodies, expanding the knowledge of Lean to systems engineering projects and large product development programs [Oppenheim, 2004, 2011]. These efforts were recognized with three Shingo Prizes, the INCOSE Fellowship, and smaller awards. The book combines these experiences into, hopefully, a product of high utility in healthcare applications.

The book assumes that the reader has a basic understanding of the critical Lean concepts of value and waste, and the skills needed to construct the Current State and Future State value stream maps in the healthcare context. If not, seminal easy-to-read texts [Graban, 2012] and [Jimmerson, 2010] are recommended.

As mentioned above, this book is limited to healthcare delivery operations conducted at the level of a local clinic, hospital, laboratory, or pharmacy. The following are examples of typical such projects:

- Reduce patient discharge time from a hospital to all destinations (home, nursing home, boarding house, hospice, street)
- Improve on-time starts in operating rooms
- Streamline patient admission from emergency department to hospital
- Reduce burnout of residents and nurses dealing with conflicting medical orders issued by operating surgeon and intensivist
- Improve scheduling of patients in a clinic
- Reduce patient throughput time in a clinic

- Reduce turnaround time of clinical tests
- Increase capacity of imaging laboratory without adding resources
- Improve turnaround time with external consultants in a clinic
- Shorten the turnaround time in a pharmacy
- Redesign instrument mounting for a new medical instrument in the ICU because the new instrument is wider than the old one and does not fit
- Change the leads on the EKG instrument that are supposed to lead to a central alarm monitoring station but do not fit the existing connectors
- Work with vendors to standardize plastic vials used in phlebotomy so they can be placed in the clinical test instrument tray directly, obviating the need for manual pouring from phlebotomy vial to instrument container
- Assure closed loop on clinical test results. If the test is positive, implement alarms for provider
- Eliminate distractions from some tasks of providers in emergency room
- Reduce transportation time of samples between collection clinics and central laboratory
- Reduce alarm fatigue in emergency department

Some projects dealing with population health, chronic care, wellness, and preventive care may have a huge impact on the patient population served and require large teams in the care delivery phase, but for the projects themselves designing the new care would still be small in terms of schedule, budget, and the project team size. Examples of such population projects involve development of effective procedures for:

- Increasing flu vaccination rate
- Decreasing disparity between Caucasian and minority populations receiving vaccinations
- Reducing obesity
- Reducing A1C in diabetic patients

This text should not be used for large healthcare projects with thousands or many hundreds of requirements, such as creation of healthcare informatics or electronic health record (EHR) software (but EHR modifications to support a clinical process improvement are included); public health and pandemic management; politics and economics of national healthcare; medical device development (but the integration of medical devices in clinical care is included); and pharmacological industry activities. These types of large projects call for full-scale traditional systems engineering [Walden et al., 2015; Sage and Rouse, 2020].

As amazing as modern healthcare is at trying to nurse all of us back to wellness and health, it is still largely a 19th-century organization: fragmented, stove-piped, provider rather than patient centric, costly and inefficient, and essentially a non-system of care. Despite frequent wrestling with inefficient workflows, healthcare continues to recruit the individuals who wish to devote their lives to helping the sick. Hopefully, the adoption of the knowledge presented in this book will help make their labors easier, more satisfying, and will be conducive to better patient care.

Bohdan W. Oppenheim
Santa Monica, California

Notes

1 Evolved from earlier Total Quality Management (TQM) [Clausing, 1994]

2 https://cse.lmu.edu/graduateprograms/hse/msstudentcapstoneprojects/

Acknowledgments

I am immensely grateful to all my graduate students in the Healthcare Systems Engineering (HSE) graduate Program at Loyola Marymount University (LMU), too numerous to mention by name, and to fellow faculty, who brought invaluable real-life healthcare examples to my attention, which stimulated many ideas presented in this work. This book is based on the research in 57 capstone projects (soon to be 100) of master's students in the LMU HSE program, which I had the honor of advising or co-advising. The full list of the projects and student names can be found on the page: https://cse.lmu.edu/graduateprograms/hse/msstudentcapstoneprojects/. I am most grateful to the colleagues at Kaiser Permanente, UCLA Health, USC Keck, Cedar Sinai, Providence St Joseph, AltaMed, and Greater VA Los Angeles for sponsoring the student projects, providing access to their medical facilities, and sharing their expertise.

My special gratitude goes to **Michael Kanter**, MD, Professor and Chair of Kaiser Permanente (KP) Medical School and former Executive Vice-President for Patient Safety and Quality at KP, for his extraordinary support in the development and operations of the HSE Program at LMU, for sharing his expertise with the author and our students on numerous occasions, and for his Foreword section in this book.

I am grateful to two faculty members of LMU HSE: **Howard Fullman**, MD, former Medical Director of Kaiser Permanente West LA Medical Center; and **Felix Ron Feinstein**, MD, Associate Medical Director, KP West LA, Ret.; as well as **Stephen Tarzynski**, MD, MPH, President of California Physicians Alliance (CaPA), for reviewing the manuscript of the book and offering valuable editing suggestions.

I am grateful to the following individuals for offering expert advice about the listed areas:

- **Hank Balch**, MD, about the sterilization of surgical instruments
- **Ron Feinstein**, MD, about OR organizations
- **Michael Kanter**, MD, about comprehensive population health methodology
- **Taylor Nornes** about Population Heath
- **Alex Quick**, MD, about the medicines used in anesthesiology
- **Paul Wafer**, CRN, about operating room challenges
- **Karen Ward**, about mental health

I am grateful to **Gabrielle Johnson**, my able Research Assistant, for help with the graphics and literature research in the book.

I am grateful to **Maria Gonzales**, graduate student of English at LMU, for her skilled help in proofreading the entire manuscript. Any remaining imperfections are my fault and not hers.

I am grateful to **Manmohan Negi** and **Marsha Hecht**, the editors at Taylor & Francis, for able removing of imperfections of my text.

Chapter 1

Introduction

Contents

1.1 Evolution of Knowledge from Systems Engineering and Lean – to Lean Healthcare Systems Engineering

The U.S. Institute of Medicine established six aims for *healthcare* quality: *safe*, *effective*, patient-centered, timely, *efficient*, and equitable [IOM, 2001]. In comparison to the other OECD countries, U.S. healthcare ranks poorly on most of these aims [Kurani, 2020]. While U.S. healthcare is known for excellent medical research, universities, technology, medical equipment, hospitals, and dedicated and well-educated professionals, these are islands of excellence drowning in the ocean of imperfect performance. The numerous reasons are well known, including lack of universal care, millions of uninsured and underinsured people, costs higher by a factor of 2–3 than the next country (UK), obesity and diabetes epidemic, lower vaccination rates, and many others [Kohn et al., 2000]. But among the reasons, one is rarely mentioned explicitly, yet it is a critical factor: fragmentation in healthcare. Healthcare delivery is the most fragmented system in our civilization. Every healthcare worker is painfully aware of the frequent miscommunications and "dropped balls" occurring in all clinical environments: between different providers; between hospital departments; between providers, patients and payers; providers and laboratories; doctors and nurses; emergency departments and hospitals; hospital and post-hospital care institutions; and this is only a short list. Fragmentation occurs in all major care delivery activities, from diagnosis and treatment, to home care, long-term care, chronic care, and preventive care. Fragmentation manifests itself in the form of miscommunications, lack of standardization, dropped balls, incompatible information, inability to access information, difficulty contacting the needed individuals, and many others. Two powerful forces contribute to the fragmentation. One is the traditional medical education which emphasizes doctors' autonomy but not the efficient system-wide workflows, in which correct information should flow reliably in a timely manner between various stakeholders and organizations involved in the patient care system. The second reason is the complex web of heterogenous health delivery institutions atomized into disjointed general and specialty clinics and hospital departments, individuals, laboratories, pharmacies, and payers. The fragmentation in the United States is particularly acute because of the lack of universal care and fragmented collection of private, employer, local, state, federal, and military organizations involved in healthcare. Due to these factors, healthcare systems have evolved to be highly stove-piped organizations optimized for the convenience of local stakeholders but not for the patient-centered care continuum. The individual organizations tend to protect their turf with functional walls, which stifle the "horizontal" flows of value that patient-centered care needs. To repeat, healthcare is probably the most fragmented of any complex civilizational system, desperately waiting for a body of knowledge focused on the integration of all relevant fragmented elements. Finally, a major milestone occurred in 2014 when the Presidential Council of Advisors on Science and Technology realized this need and issued an appeal to systems engineers to come to the rescue of healthcare [PCAST, 2014].

The term **Systems Engineering (SE)** is somewhat misleading as it conjures images of engineering and mathematical formulas. Not so. It is a historical term. The discipline of *Systems Engineering* (SE) was created by Si Ramo and Dean Woldridge in 1954 to help with the development of ballistic missiles, which had to work unconditionally [Jacobson, 2001]. Ramo and Woldridge realized that those missiles are too complex and too dangerous to rely on individual engineering disciplines of mechanical, aerodynamic, electrical, propulsion, and others, in isolation from one another [Brown, 2009]. They understood that complex systems usually fail at the interdisciplinary interfaces rather than within single-discipline elements. The individual elements going into a system may be perfectly designed by best disciplinary experts, but they fail the assembly into the system. The individual elements do not fit together physically, functionally, electronically, or in terms of human interactions – because disciplinary engineers did not understand the interfaces between the disciplines or the people. Thus, some new process had to be invented to assure perfect integration of the elements across all interfaces. The word "engineering" in the name is historical, originating from the fact that the process was applied to engineering systems. In healthcare environment that word is somewhat unfortunate and misleading, scaring healthcare professionals with mental images of mathematical formulas. In fact, there is very little engineering in SE, even less mathematics[1]; it is more like a rigorous logical process for managing the creation and flow of information throughout the project. Our definition of SE is:

BOX 1.1 DEFINITION OF SYSTEMS ENGINEERING

SE is a rigorous time-proven process of management and coordination of all relevant technical details and elements, and strong focus on the system integration and life-cycle performance. It is a process of rigorous integration of complex fragmented elements so that they work together as a system, perfectly, as intended!

The SE process is not derived from natural sciences or mathematics. It is a heuristic body of knowledge more akin to Project Management (PM) but focused on managing flow of information in fragmented systems while PM tends to focus on management of resources, but there is some overlap between PM and SE[2].

Since the beginning in the 1950s, during the next 70 years SE was used mostly in large engineering programs in defense, aerospace, infrastructure, energy, and automotive programs (henceforth just called "engineering"). The defense context of SE is important for our considerations because large defense programs funded and led the evolution of systems engineering. Besides technical capabilities, such programs are driven by powerful political and lobbying forces whose main objectives are jobs, cost-plus contracting, long-term profits, and risk aversion. In this environment, process efficiencies and streamlining have been a low priority. It is not unusual for a defense program to start with several thousand top-level requirements, each of which is often divided into about 10 lower-level requirements [Carter, 2010]. Consequently, the biggest portion of a typical defense SE effort is spent on management of this huge number of requirements: formulating, iterating, deconflicting, clarifying, modifying, and verifying [Oppenheim, 2011]. The team involved in the execution of a typical defense development program involves hundreds of companies distributed nationally and even internationally with hundreds of thousands of stakeholders, plus a significant number of military or NASA workers. A typical large program lasts tens of years and creates hundreds of thousands or millions of program documents that comprise program requirements management and related activities, and subsequent system design [Carter, 2010]. To integrate and coordinate such vast programs, SE evolved into an inefficient bureaucracy of requirements management. Eric Honor, the 1997 INCOSE[3] President named it "the bureaucracy of artifacts" [Honour, 2010].

A major development in the field of SE started in the early 2000s, with the adoption of a computerized representation of program requirements, documents, and models describing various system characteristics and elements. Named Model Based Systems Engineering (MBSE), it soon became a popular tool in requirements management, as it eliminated bulky paper documents with well-organized data structures. It was crowned in INCOSE's 2007 vision statement which promoted ubiquitous[4] use of MBSE in all programs by 2020 [INCOSE, 2007]. Indeed, many systems engineers practicing in large technology programs became enthusiastic about MBSE. But this was also the beginning of a serious "cognitive divorce" between the mainstream SE users and healthcare practitioners, as follows.

After the 2014 PCAST appeal to systems engineers to come to the rescue of healthcare, and seeing the huge size of the U.S. healthcare industry (at $3 trillion, three times larger than defense and by far the largest segment of U.S. economy), systems engineers eagerly anticipated similarly big opportunities in healthcare. Numerous initiatives were attempted to apply SE in healthcare delivery projects using MBSE. The author participated in several INCOSE Healthcare Working Group conferences [INCOSE HWG, 2020] in which healthcare executives described their needs and systems engineers presented the MBSE approach, resulting in a decidedly inadequate mutual match. The disappointments were driven by two reasons. First, the funding: large defense programs are funded by the federal government, while typical healthcare delivery projects focus on improving some aspect of workflow or care in a local setting, e.g., in a local clinic, hospital, laboratory, or pharmacy. Secondly, typical projects in healthcare are several orders of magnitude smaller than defense programs. The following are examples of typical projects:

- Reduce patient discharge time from a hospital to all destinations (home, nursing home, boarding house, hospice, street)
- Improve on-time starts in operating rooms
- Streamline patient admission from emergency department to hospital
- Reduce burnout of residents and nurses dealing with conflicting medical orders issued by operating surgeon and intensivist
- Improve scheduling of patients in a clinic
- Reduce patient throughput time in a clinic
- Reduce turnaround time of clinical tests
- Increase capacity of imaging laboratory without adding resources
- Improve turnaround time with external consultants in a clinic
- Shorten the turnaround time in a pharmacy
- Redesign instrument mounting for a new medical instrument in the ICU because the new instrument is wider than the old one and does not fit
- Change the leads on the EKG instrument which are supposed to lead to a central alarm monitoring station, but they do not fit the existing connectors
- Work with vendors to standardize plastic vials used in phlebotomy so that they can be placed in the clinical test instrument tray directly, obviating the need for manual pouring from phlebotomy vial to instrument container
- Assure closed loop on clinical test results. If the test is positive implement alarms for provider
- Eliminate distractions from some tasks of providers in emergency room
- Reduce transportation time of samples between collection clinics and central laboratory
- Reduce alarm fatigue in emergency department

Some population health projects dealing with chronic care, wellness, and preventive care may have a huge impact on the patient population served, and require large teams in the care delivery phase, but the projects themselves designing the new care would still be small in terms of schedule, budget, and the project team size. Examples of such population projects involve development of effective procedures for:

■ Increasing flu vaccination rate
■ Decreasing disparity between Caucasian and minority populations receiving vaccinations
■ Reducing obesity
■ Reducing A1C in diabetic patients

This text should not be used for large healthcare projects with thousands or many hundreds of requirements, such as creation of healthcare informatics or electronic health record (EHR) software (but EHR modifications to support a clinical process improvement are included); public health and pandemic management; politics and economics of universal healthcare; medical device development (but the integration of medical devices in clinical care is included); and pharmacological industry activities. These types of large projects call for full-scale traditional systems engineering [Walden et al., 2015; Sage, 2020].

The typical healthcare delivery projects involve a few individuals working for a few weeks or months with small budgets or even no explicit budgets (working as a part of their regular duties), and the projects start with only a few (or even only one) requirement. Table 1.1 compares the typical scope of such projects to defense programs.

Table 1.1   Scale of Healthcare versus Defense Programs

	Typical Healthcare Delivery Project	Typical Defense Program
Number of Requirements	Under 10	1000–100,000
Budgets	$10,000–$100,000	$billions
Number of employees involved	Under 10	10,000s–100,000s
Project duration	Weeks to months	Decades
Driving incentive	Streamline a workflow or care in a local clinic or hospital or lab	Cost-plus federal funding and jobs

The bifurcation of interests should not come as a surprise when we observe the divergent incentives (see Table 1.1). Defense programs involve tens of thousands of requirements, while healthcare projects involve one to a few requirements. The application of MBSE to only a few requirements would be a monstrous overkill and cause unacceptable cost increase, requiring a long learning curve to master MBSE because healthcare workers tend to lack the prerequisite technical background. And the benefits would be negligible. This dramatic difference in project scope was the source of the main disappointment on the part of many traditional systems engineers who wanted to undertake healthcare delivery projects, and on the part of healthcare managers eager for help from systems engineers. We hope to radically change this situation with the present text. The following box describes the aim of the book.

The aim of the book is to demonstrate that:

- **Healthcare projects critically need the systems engineering process.**
- **Systems engineering can bring extraordinary practical benefits to healthcare projects.**
- **Most healthcare projects need only a simplified version of systems engineering, dramatically reduced in complexity relative to the traditional version used in large engineering programs. This text presents a version of the systems engineering process focused on healthcare and strongly simplified using the wisdom of Lean thinking, named LHSE.**
- **No prior engineering background is needed to use the LHSE process.**

The term "**Lean**" in the context of work was coined by [Womack et al., 1990] who published the seminal bestseller *The Machine that Changed the World*, which described the astonishingly efficient Toyota Production System, followed by another bestseller *Lean Thinking* [Womack, 1993], which explained the Lean work organization in detail. Soon Lean evolved into several non-manufacturing disciplines, including healthcare. The formative book *Lean Hospitals* [Graban, 2012] demonstrated the power of Lean in streamlining hospital operations. Lean has become an established paradigm for effective removal of waste and streamlining of delivery operations in hospitals, clinics, and ancillary departments. We call this approach Lean Healthcare

(LH). As effective as it is in fighting waste, LH did not address the powerful potential of SE for integrating fragmented healthcare elements. **Our aim is to integrate LH with SE, or more precisely with Lean SE.**

We use Lean to reduce waste and streamline work processes. A twin body of knowledge called Six Sigma [Harry and Schroeder, 2000] is used to elevate the process bottlenecks and imperfections. Industrial experience indicates that both are needed: Lean to promote process speed and Six Sigma to remove the speed stifling bottlenecks. The integrated body of knowledge is often called Lean Six Sigma [Wedgewood, 2007]. In this book, consistent with frequent industrial practice, for brevity we use the term **Lean,** but we include in it the integrated practices of **Lean Six Sigma**.

The adoption of Lean into SE started with Air Force General James Ferguson who was in charge of procuring military aircraft [Murman et al., 2002]. Impressed by the two books by Womack et al., he initiated a consortium called *Lean Advancement Initiative[5](LAI)* [Murman et al., 2002] based at MIT and intended to adopt Lean into military product development programs, which include strong SE elements. In 2004, the LAI invited universities into the network, starting with LMU in Los Angeles in the charter role. In 2006, the present author initiated a new Working Group at INCOSE devoted to the application of Lean to Systems Engineering, which grew to be the largest Working Group in INCOSE, with over 250 members. During the following seven years, numerous books, journal articles, and conference presentations were published creating and expanding the new body of knowledge called Lean Systems Engineering [Oppenheim, 2011], and were rewarded with several Shingo Prizes. In 2012, a joint project of MIT, INCOSE, and Project Management Institute published an influential work, *The Guide to Lean Enablers for Managing Engineering Programs* [Oehmen, 2012], integrating Lean SE with Project Management. The culmination of this effort was the insertion of a chapter on Lean SE into the INCOSE Handbook [Walden et al., 2015, chapter on Lean by Oppenheim]. This became an important milestone, namely a formal adoption of Lean as an inherent, although optional, part of the SE process.

Soon after the PCAST 2014 appeal, the present author created a new branch of the existing SE graduate program at LMU, named Healthcare Systems Engineering (HSE). Executives of Kaiser Permanente (who participated in the PCAST deliberations) and colleagues from the MIT LAI provided immense help in the creation of a comprehensive HSE curriculum. Because of a strong involvement of the faculty in the Lean SE work, both at MIT LAI and INCOSE, during the previous 15 years, Lean Healthcare was made a strong component of the LMU HSE program. In the program, graduate students study a broad range of healthcare challenges and solutions, ending with a comprehensive capstone project. Besides the ability to improve healthcare processes, all such projects must demonstrate competence of the SE process in healthcare, Lean healthcare, and medical ethics applied to a particular healthcare situation. At the time of this writing, 57 projects (soon to be 100) have been completed at several California sites of Kaiser Permanente, Cedar Sinai, Providence St. Joseph, UCLA Health, Veterans Administration, USC Keck/County Hospitals, AltaMed, and smaller facilities [https://cse.lmu.edu/graduateprograms/hse/msstudentcapstoneprojects/]. This author served as mentor and advisor or co-advisor in most of the projects. The present text represents a synthesis of the knowledge gleaned from these projects.

The main conclusion from these projects is that healthcare needs a simplified SE process, stripped of all elements which evolved to deal with the massive size of teams, budgets, and technical complexity of defense programs, and which would be wasteful in healthcare delivery operations. Healthcare needs SE to provide logical rigor when integrating fragmented pieces, an assurance of high reliability, and it must be delivered in a manner which is user-friendly for healthcare stakeholders, supporting and facilitating their work without adding burden or cost. We named this simplified process **Lean Healthcare Systems Engineering (LHSE)**, and defined it as follows:

BOX 1.2 DEFINITION OF LEAN HEALTHCARE SYSTEMS ENGINEERING (LHSE)

Lean Healthcare Systems Engineering (LHSE) is a simplified SE process of integrating and streamlining projects involved in improving healthcare workflows and care in all clinical environments, such as clinics and hospitals of all types, including emergency departments, operating suites, and ancillary departments; imaging and clinical laboratories; pharmacies; telemedicine; population health; preventive and chronic care; and home and nursing care. The LHSE process contains only those steps which are critical to project success, free of the burdens, constructs, and procedures which, while possibly augmenting the traditional systems engineering elegance, are not essential to the project success. LHSE is the logically rigorous process that integrates all activities so that the intended outcomes (workflow, diagnosis, treatment, cure, wellness, or illness prevention) are assured. LHSE relies on Lean Healthcare to identify waste and streamline operations. LHSE relies on SE to create and integrate the needed building blocks of the LHSE process.

Figure 1.1 illustrates the integration of different knowledge domains into LHSE.

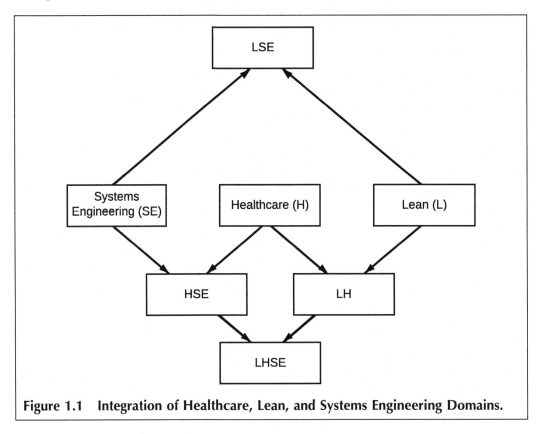

Figure 1.1 Integration of Healthcare, Lean, and Systems Engineering Domains.

In summary, the contributions of the above knowledge domains to LHSE are as follows:

- **Healthcare (H)** delivery system is the client domain, providing a need, or a challenge to create or improve a healthcare workflow or care.
- **Lean (L)** helps to identify and delete waste and provides the means to streamline a given process.
- **Lean Healthcare (LH)** provides Lean approach specialized for healthcare delivery applications.
- **Systems Engineering (SE)** provides a rigorous logical process for managing information in programs and projects and assuring integration of fragmented interdisciplinary system elements, as well as unconditional system performance.
- **Lean Systems Engineering (LSE)** assures that only truly needed elements of SE will be used, that they will be used only to the degree

needed, be user-friendly, and that they will be free of bureaucratic overhead.

■ **Healthcare Systems Engineering (HSE)** is the application of SE to healthcare delivery operations. Adopting the "defense" version of SE is not recommended, as it would result in waste, bureaucracy, large teams, long schedules, and high costs.

■ **Lean Healthcare Systems Engineering (LHSE)** introduced in this book is the Lean version of Healthcare Systems Engineering, leading to well-integrated rigorous and effective solutions to healthcare delivery challenges. LHSE was created to provide the optimum utility to healthcare stakeholders, applicable to a comprehensive class of healthcare delivery systems.

Two terms are often confused: the **systems engineering (SE) body of knowledge** [Sage, 2020] and **the process of SE** [Walden et al., 2015]. The former is a huge body of knowledge broadly used to study complex systems. The SE process is a part of that knowledge. It is a step-by-step technique of executing SE in projects and programs. We have a similar situation with the term Healthcare Systems Engineering. It has two meanings. First, it represents a huge body of knowledge including subjects such as health IT, patient safety systems, population health, public health, health analytics, Lean healthcare, modeling in healthcare, medical device systems, etc. This knowledge is taught at a graduate level in academic programs typically called Healthcare Systems Engineering[6] and published, among others, in Transactions on HSE [IISE Transactions]. **The second meaning is that HSE is a process, a step-by-step technique of executing healthcare projects. This book is limited to the process, specifically to the Lean-inspired process of executing the Healthcare Systems Engineering (LHSE) projects.**

Since medical professions have been focused on medicine rather than formal project management, literature is silent about any formal workflow or care improvement project process. We can only surmise that the dominant process was "managing by instinct." In recent years, project management became the dominant methodology, particularly in the academic Master of Healthcare Administration programs. At the time of this writing, SE process is rather new to many healthcare institutions. One aim of this book is to convince the readers that SE adds the needed logical rigor, consistency, and repeatability; integrates fragmented elements; guides users toward better choices of alternatives; reduces risks; formulates disciplined requirements; verifies and validates the results; and provides significantly better results overall[7] but that it should be practiced in the LHSE version rather than as the classical "big guerilla" SE.

As already mentioned, the LHSE process is generic, applicable to practically any healthcare project on the scale of a clinic, hospital, including OR and ED, lab, or pharmacy, or population health. The reader will find sample project summaries tabularized as Lean Enablers in Chapter 3 of the present book.

1.2 Book Organization

This book is organized into two parts, as follows:

1. Chapter 2 describes the LHSE process step by step, as it should be followed in all projects. This part of the book can be used as a "user-friendly" manual and reference text for the LHSE process.
2. Chapter 3 is intended as a reference text for the first major product created using the LHSE process, namely tabularized summaries of representative projects in healthcare delivery applications in specific clinical environments: clinics and hospitals, including emergency departments and operating rooms; imaging and clinical laboratories, ancillary departments, pharmacies, and population health. For each environment, we list typical challenges (problems, inefficiencies, frustrations, wastes, etc.) and propose LHSE solutions (recommended corrective actions). In this part, we adopted a standardized tabular layout, listing the environment (hospital, etc.), defining the system of interest and key elements, stakeholders, goals, proposed LHSE solutions, risks, and expected benefits. Key elements of the literature published on the given topic are identified in the tables, although at the time of this writing, none includes the LHSE ideas. Hopefully, these summaries will make the life of healthcare project professionals much easier than traditional methods. Because the proposed solutions are based on Lean Thinking, always reducing waste and streamlining operations, they can be regarded as Lean Enablers for Healthcare. The Lean Enablers approach to challenges has been well established in literature [Oppenheim 2004, 2011; Oehmen, 2012].

As mentioned earlier, the Lean Enablers tables in Chapter 3 were inspired by the author's personal experience gained from the 57 projects mentioned above. An interesting consistent observation from these projects executed in eight medical institutions is that the challenges are remarkably similar among the institutions, and therefore the corrective actions listed should apply to all of them, upon only minor customization. This observation was confirmed by many practicing healthcare managers. Thus, Chapter 3 of the book is organized into Lean Enablers for different clinical environments (clinic, hospital, etc.), listing typical challenges and typical solution ideas. The intent is to make this book directly usable and user-friendly to healthcare professionals as they toil creating and improving care processes and outcomes.

The remainder of the book is organized as follows. Continuing with Chapter 1, lessons on the benefits of using systems engineering are covered briefly in the following section. The classical systems engineering process called the "V" is described next, and it is compared to the LHSE version of the "V."

In Chapter 2, we describe the four phases of LHSE process: Background, Analysis of Current State, Design of Future State, and Implementation, respectively.

Chapter 3 contains the Lean Enablers, with tabular summaries of healthcare challenges and LHSE ideas for improvements. We first present the layout of the subsequent tables, and then list the detailed Enablers in the following order:

3.1 Clinics
3.2 Hospitals
3.3 Emergency departments
3.4 Operating rooms (suites)
3.5 Pharmacies
3.6 Imaging (radiology) laboratories
3.7 Clinical laboratories
3.8 Population health

The Appendix presents two other SE processes. The first is the comprehensive iterative methodology for systems engineering projects created by the UK Royal Academy of Engineering. The second is the classical SE process used in large engineering programs. These processes are included for intellectual curiosity but are not recommended to replace LHSE presented in Chapter 2.

Glossary of Terms, References, Author's Biography, and Index complete the book.

When describing various project activities, the author takes the liberty of using the grammatical form "we." This should not be taken as the "royal or papal *We*," but rather as an indication that the present author likes to consider himself a part of your team, offering suggestions and teaching steps.

1.3 Is SE Process a Good Investment of Project Budget?

Eric Honor [2010] conducted an extensive study of the benefits of systems engineering to programs. While his study was limited to large, mostly government-funded defense and aerospace programs, he concluded that the most successful programs spent about 15% of their total budgets on systems engineering. At 15% systems engineering provides the most predictable program cost and schedule. See Figure 1.2.

With two exceptions, all programs included in Honour's study used some systems engineering. The two exceptions are illustrated as two dots on the left vertical axes on the two graphs of Figure 1.2. These dots illustrate that both cost and schedule were worse by 60% and 80%, respectively, from the optimal values of 15% of the engineering effort.

In the programs studies by Honour, a full-blown engineering version of the SE process was used. Our LHSE is a dramatically simpler version. Therefore, the "extra budget" spent on LHSE will be minimal, recovered by better execution of the project. Anecdotal understanding by the present author based on 57 healthcare projects is that LHSE makes the projects less open-ended and less iterative, and more rigorous in formulating problems, goals, requirements, alternatives, architectures, risks, verification, and validation, as well as implementations. Reducing project iterations saves costs. The risks of using LHSE are zero. The investment of effort is the familiarization of the material in Chapter 2. Project participants who use LHSE find that they can devote more effort to the healthcare subject matter and less to wondering aimlessly through project steps. Basically, LHSE provides a solid process, a framework for carrying just about any healthcare project. A few of the author's graduate students who first completed

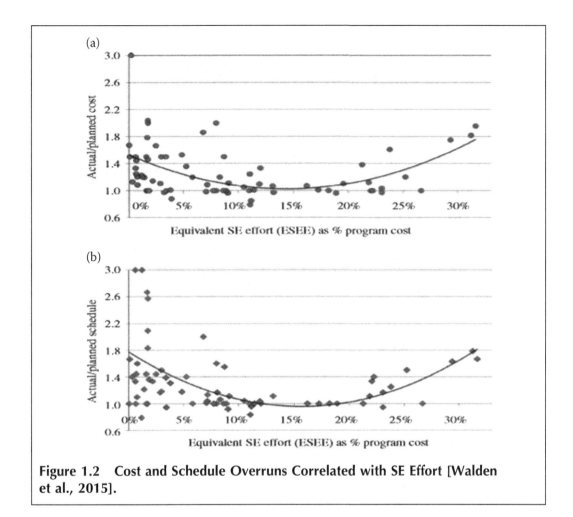

Figure 1.2 Cost and Schedule Overruns Correlated with SE Effort [Walden et al., 2015].

most of their projects without using LHSE, and then discovered that they were required to use it, and did so, commented "I wish I had used LHSE from scratch; it benefitted the project quality so much."

1.4 Classical Systems Engineering "V" Process and the LHSE "V" Process

Figure 1.3 illustrates the classical systems engineering process as the so-called "V" [Wikipedia, 2020; Walden et al., 2015]. It shows the major project/program process activities versus time. The activities will be described in detail in Chapter 2 of this book, but most terms are self-explanatory. Large engineering programs, particularly large defense programs, spend most of their systems engineering time on requirements management: formulating, collecting, analyzing, iterating, and changing requirements, as well as on test and verification.

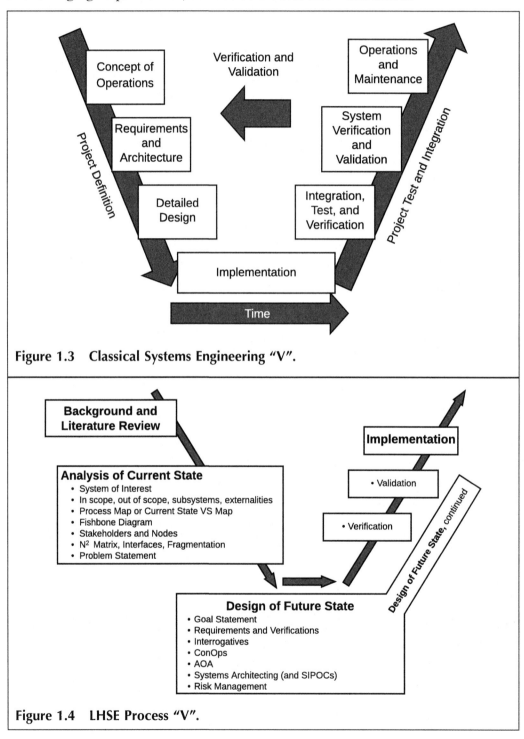

Figure 1.3   Classical Systems Engineering "V".

Figure 1.4   LHSE Process "V".

The LHSE process is shown in Figure 1.4. It has four main phases: Background, Analysis of Current State, Design of Future State, and Implementation. They are described in Chapter 2.

Comparing Figures 1.3 and 1.4, we see that the term "Implementation" has a different position on the charts. It also has a different meaning. In classical systems engineering, in Figure 1.3, it denotes the program phase in which we perform detailed design, subcontracting, production, and manufacturing of the system hardware, software, and logistics. In contrast, in healthcare delivery operations, we do not produce hardware or software[8], but rather methods, procedures, standards, checklists, agreements, and others that represent an improvement of a workflow or care, or a creation of a new healthcare process. The system that we create deals with improved, better integrated flow of information in human interactions. These systems are created in the LHSE project phase called Design of Future State, which is distinct from Implementation. In LHSE, Implementation and operationalization are performed as the last step of the project, as shown in Figure 1.4.

Notes

1 Some exotic branches of systems engineering use mathematics [Sage and Rouse, 2020], but these are ignored here, as they are of little practical use in healthcare operations.

2 Modern trend [Rebentisch, 2017] is to integrate both SE and PM processes into one project management process, but this is outside of the scope of this text.

3 INCOSE is the International Council for Systems Engineering, the main professional society of systems engineers.

4 David Long, 2014–15 INCOSE President and the owner of a company producing important MBSE tools, in his written communication to this author, stated that MBSE should not be regarded as panacea to all projects and programs and the term "ubiquities" should be applied judiciously.

5 The original name was *Lean Aircraft Initiative* and it focused on military aircraft production. Soon the consortium expanded onto other aerospace systems and was renamed *Lean Aerospace Initiative*, and after other military branches joined, it was again renamed *Lean Advancement Initiative,* all keeping the same acronym LAI.

6 For example, see the LMU graduate program https://cse.lmu.edu/graduateprograms/hse/; or the *Journal of Healthcare Systems Engineering*.

7 Formal evidence for this claim is lacking. However, in many of the 57 projects in six different healthcare institutions in which the author was involved, he had a chance to observe the initial attempts without SE, and subsequent rigorous

application of the SE process, with the results vastly better in the latter one. Without SE, projects tend to be governed by instinct, experience of providers, and tend to be strongly influenced by the hierarchy gradient. The subsequent addition of the SE process significantly improved the project rigor, objectivity, and quality of the results.

8 Some projects may require small modifications and customizations of the EHR system.

Chapter 2

Lean Healthcare Systems Engineering (LHSE) Process

Contents

LHSE projects have four distinct phases: background, analysis of current state, design of future state, and implementation[1]. They are discussed in turn.

2.1 Background

Starting a new project with a description of the project background provides an important common context for current and future workers and stakeholders. The background section should include a description of the project environment. We should also identify the project location, for example, clinic department X in hospital Y in the medical institution Z, located in town Q, as well as the main characteristics relevant to the project, such as the number and demographics of patients served, the number and type of employees of different levels, relevant union organizations represented, ancillary facilities, and cooperating vendors. We should also state any applicable regulatory and resource constraints (e.g., budget and available staff), if relevant.

We should name the reason(s) why this project is undertaken. However, it is important that we do not "jump the gun" and attempt to state the project goals right away – that will be done in the next project phase, Analysis of Current State. In the Background phase, at most we may wish to state an initial reason for the project, for example, "shorten the discharge time of patients from the hospital." At this phase, we normally do not have sufficient evidence to state the project goal precisely. It is only after we analyze the Current State in detail, interview the stakeholders, and perform benchmarking to other like units that we will have sufficient knowledge to do so. The reader is reminded that the LHSE process requires logical rigor, and "not jumping the gun" is a part of the rigor.

Next, we briefly present opportunities for improvements or new solutions. We may describe the current challenges: frustrations, burnout, gaps in quality, safety, cost, process time, fragmentation, miscommunications, etc. The terms and abbreviations not commonly known should be explained. If applicable, we should cite the existing literature and summarize former/similar solutions or past attempts to deal with the challenge. Healthcare literature is vast, problems tend to be common, and it is highly likely that others have addressed a similar problem. We need to understand what has been done by others to build on it rather than "reinvent the wheel."

Box 2.1 provides an example of the Background information to include. The example deals with the project of reducing the time of patient discharge from a hospital to local Skilled Nursing Facilities (SNFs). For brevity, we are omitting details, and only indicating the topics.

BOX 2.1 SAMPLE INFORMATION TO INCLUDE IN THE BACKGROUND SECTION OF THE PROJECT

- In hospital X in town Z, which is a part of healthcare system Y, the process of discharging patients from the hospital to four Skilled Nursing Facilities (SNFs) takes 2–3 times the average time in competing facilities in the same location, dealing with the same SNFs, which is two hours.
- The scope of hospital services is [describe].
- During last year, an average of 3 patients were referred to an SNF in each 24-hour day, with a maximum of 6 and a minimum of 0.
- Frustrations include an excessively bureaucratic process of discharging the patients. On the hospital side, the coordination among the discharge nurses, case manager, continued care coordinator, and insurance clerk is less than perfect and causes delays. For each patient, the negotiations with several SNFs start anew, one SNF at a time. The SNFs appear to pose arbitrary and varying medical criteria for patient admission, trying to select the healthiest patients only.
- The delays in discharge penalize the hospital with excessive bed occupancy costs and hinder the capacity which could be used for new patients. The cost of keeping a patient in the hospital bed after the discharge order has been issued is $W per hour, and in the discharge lounge it is $WW per hour, but the discharge lounge is only used for healthier patients – those who do not require a hospital bed or nursing help.
- Summary of best relevant solutions from literature.

In the spirit of Lean, we must balance the amount of information provided in the Background phase with the waste of information, overproduction, and over processing. The right amount is that which facilitates subsequent communications between project stakeholders and sponsors, avoids miscommunication, and promotes project success and implementation. A typical project will have 3–20 slides devoted to the Background.

2.2 Analysis of Current State (AoCS)

The main objective of the project phase called Analysis of Current State (AoCS) is to acquire perfect understanding of the current state and gather evidence with data [Balestracci, 2015]. Here we seek evidence of the problem to address, diving deeply into the current challenges, wastes, and frustrations, and seeking to understand root causes of problems. The last step of the AoCS is the Problem Statement, which will serve in the next phase of the project: Design of Future State, as the starting point for designing the solution with a high degree of rigor. The AoCS should not be confused with the Background phase, which is just that: a general description of the environment under study, or with the Design of Future State phase, where we create the needed solution. To avoid unnecessary iterations and confusion, the three phases should not be comingled.

The AoCS is quite open-ended in terms of the format and tools used. Typically, we use tools from several disciplines, as applicable, as convenient, and as useful: healthcare management; systems engineering; Lean and Six Sigma; Quality, and Plan, Do, Study, Act (PDSA) methodology; Statistical Process Control (SPC), Theory of Constraints, and other methods to study variability, and project management. If needed, we may have to bring in expertise from medicine, IT, engineering, and law. The overriding objective is to gain the needed knowledge of our system rather than discipline purity. The subsequent sections describe some of the more popular tools taken from the domains of systems engineering and Lean Six Sigma, but they should not be interpreted as exclusive or mandatory. This open-ended character of the AoCS may appear to contradict the LHSE rigor, which we emphasize so heavily. Indeed, the rigor should come in the depth of understanding of our problem and the formulation of the Problem Statement rather than the type of tools used toward this goal. The reader will find a higher degree of tools rigor in the next project phase, Design of Future State.

2.2.1 Stakeholders, System of Interest, Project Scope, and Externalities

The first step in the AoCS is to select our "System of Interest (SoI)," project scope, and system elements including both human stakeholders and non-human nodes, for example, the Electronic Health Record (EHR). These selections should be performed early in the project because the choice will affect our subsequent in-scope and out-of-scope project activities, the level of effort, project duration, and budget. The selections of system, stakeholders, and scope are related because changing one affects the others. The selection may be iterative; we start with one of the three, whichever is easiest, then identify the others; and consider the effect of our choice on project effort, budget, and duration. We should not hesitate to change the choice if we see a better one. Once the SoI has been defined, we can then indicate external systems interacting with (affecting or being affected by) our SoI, or "externalities." Figure 2.1 illustrates the SoI, its elements, and in-scope activities as well as externalities for the project of patient discharge from a hospital. Major interfaces (interactions) are shown as thick arrows. In this example, they represent negotiations between the entities shown.

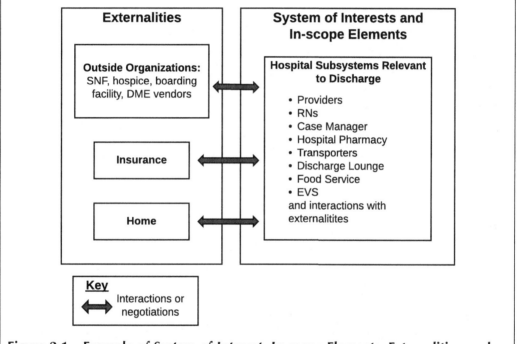

Figure 2.1   Example of System of Interest, In-scope Elements, Externalities, and Interactions (Interfaces) for a Project of Patient Discharge from a Hospital.

We should be careful with the selection of our SoI size. It is intuitively obvious that selecting too big a system leads to excessive project size, unaffordable costs, and duration. Many projects failed because too big a system was selected. Too small a system risks missing important system characteristics or interfaces. The balance must be right. We should not hesitate to change it if we are not satisfied with the current attempt before we move on with the project.

When selecting the SoI size, we are dealing with competing pressures. One is the size of healthcare economy. The entire U.S. healthcare is a vast system of systems involving almost 20% of GDP, 24% of government spending, and 11% of the national employment (disregarding self-employed individuals)

[Noon, 2020]. Every single person present in the country is a current or potential patient[2]. Among the numerous ways to categorize healthcare stakeholders, both human and functional, this author finds the following useful:

- Patients, potential patients, family, home caregivers (that includes everybody present in the country!)
- Providers and support employees (doctors, assistants, and nurses of all ranks, including residents, medical students, technicians, administrators, and support staff)
- Care organizations: general and specialty clinics, hospitals, operating rooms, emergency departments, ambulances and fire departments, imaging and clinical laboratories, pharmacies, skilled nursing facilities, hospices, boarding facilities, home care institutions, and supporting staff
- Medical equipment makers and users, and durable medical equipment (DME) vendors
- Pharmaceutical industry
- Research: Academia, National Institute of Health (NIH), Center for Disease Control (CDC)
- International bodies, for example, World Health Organization (WHO), EHR standardization committees
- Payers (insurances, employers, and governments)
- Employers
- Governments (federal, state, local, and international organizations)
- Military Health and Veteran Administration (VA)
- Regulatory bodies and professional societies
- First Responders: fire departments, ambulances, college medical emergency teams, etc.
- Stakeholders involved in large emergency events (mass accidents, earthquakes, fires, floods, wars, and riots)
- Phases of care: medical diagnosis (Dx), treatment (Tx), wellness and preventive care, chronic care, geriatric, and palliative care
- Public health institutions and staff, including pandemic preparations, logistics, and care
- Software: EHR systems, healthcare informatics makers and users, and a rich and expanding menu of applications

It is a vast system indeed, with overlapping areas. Even though one could perform an intellectual exercise finding relationships among any or all of these stakeholders, it is intuitively obvious that such an approach to a specific local project improving a workflow or care element would be preposterously excessive.

Another pressure when selecting the SoI size is the project funding source. When projects are funded by governments, powerful incentives exist to include as many aspects of the SoI as possible. As discussed in Section 1.1, the frequent "bigger is better" trend in the defense industry made classical SE too inefficient to be of interest to healthcare.

The third pressure comes from Systems Thinking, a prerequisite and important corollary of SE, the body of knowledge that teaches us to always think in the larger context, to think of emerging properties and unintended consequences, and of far-reaching interactions within and outside of our SoI[3]. This approach certainly applies to national health initiatives such as public health, designs of universal healthcare, and many other applications, but we need to be careful not to spread the thinking too wide when we manage local projects improving care workflow or quality.

So we are dealing with this inherent but healthy conflict between several pressures to spread our thinking wide, and Lean thinking, which promotes the idea of the teams of active project stakeholders being as small and only as absolutely required for the effective solution and no more. Where is "the happy medium"? In this text, the following approach is suggested:

> **When scoping an LHSE project, we should be guided by common sense and work experience, as well as Lean thinking. Common sense and experience help us understand the problem, identify opportunities for improvement, and suggest relevant stakeholders and system elements. Lean directs us to include only what is critical to the project success and consider everything else as waste.**

Typically, LHSE projects will be local, executed within a hospital, clinic, or ancillary department (such as a lab) or a few cooperating departments, with only a few active stakeholders participating in the project. If the given local project turns out successful, the results (methods, procedures, standards, checklists, software, training) should be shared with other sister organizations to promote the highest quality throughout the entire institution and avoid reinventing the wheel. A sample list of projects that are perfectly suited for the LHSE approach was listed in Chapter 1. Chapter 3 of the book contains a more complete list.

Often, only one person executes the project and interacts with others only when needed. Such projects tend to have the schedule measured in weeks or months, budgets in the low $10k range (or none, if executed as a part of regular work), and only a few top-level requirements, sometimes as few as one, e.g., "The new process shall reduce the discharge time from hospital by 30% before a specific date."

As mentioned in Chapter 1, some projects dealing with population health, such as chronic care, wellness, and preventive care, may have a huge impact on the patient population served, and require large teams in the care delivery phase, but the projects themselves designing the new care would still be small in terms of schedule, budget, and the project team size.

One group of stakeholders requires a special mention, namely the individuals whose interests may be contrary to the project goals. If we exclude such individuals from project stakeholders, they may slow down the project, even disrupt the results. For example, in the project attempting to reduce the discharge time of patients from a hospital, success depends on the willingness of cooperating outside institutions (SNFs, boarding facilities, hospices) to periodically negotiate patient acceptance criteria and standards, so that subsequent individual patient placement would be almost automatic, requiring no separate negotiations, subject only to space availability. Therefore, managers of these cooperating institutions should be included as stakeholders. Another example: in a semi-closed ICU, a conflict between the surgical team and the ICU intensivists on how to treat a post-op patient is not uncommon, resulting in frequently changing orders for treatment. The conflict tends to put inordinate pressure on the residents and nurses, causing burnout. So, in a project dealing with ICU improvements, we should include a representative attending MDs from both, OR and ICU sides, to motivate them to come to an agreement on how to resolve the differences, working as a single team for the good of the patient. The patient-centric principle of medical ethics is of great help when resolving such conflicts. Another example is frequent apparent conflict between unions and management (called "apparent" because it so appears until an agreement is reached, at which point it may become a win-win success). Both should be represented on a single team.

2.2.2 Fragmentation and the N^2 Matrix

Fragmentation is recognized as one of the biggest evils of healthcare [Elhauge, 2010] in all healthcare systems. For example, the U.K. socialized medical system suffers from it as much as the market-based U.S. system [Dodds, 2018].

LHSE manages fragmentation by identifying and fixing all imperfect interfaces between the relevant fragmented elements within the SoI and those with externalities. At our disposal we have one of the most powerful tools of systems engineering called the N^2 (pronounced N squared) matrix, where N is the number of elements in the system. The selection of N elements of our system is often not obvious when dealing with human beings and organizations. One of the critical questions that comes up in every project is what level of granularity should be used when listing the elements. Too high a granularity will yield a large N and the N^2 number will be so large that it becomes unmanageable, drowning the solution in irrelevant details. Too few elements may hide important interfaces. For example, should we look at a single combined interface between a provider and a clinical lab performing the ordered blood test, or should we also include the provider's nurse who prints the lab orders and hands them to the patient? Should we treat the clinical lab as a single element or break it down as several, perhaps tens of interacting individuals handling the samples being analyzed? Even in simple projects the variety of elements that may contribute to fragmentation is huge, including:

- Patient, family, caregivers
- Healthcare staff: different doctors, nurses, technicians, administrators, insurance clerk
- Organizations: departments, labs, pharmacies
- Software used: EHRs, other Healthcare Informatics tools
- Tests applied
- Equipment used
- Applicable rules, laws, and regulations

and this is a short list. Each element larger than just an individual human being can be mentally broken into its constituent individuals but doing it in a healthcare project often leads to an absurd problem size. Again, we need to be guided by common sense and Lean: include only as many relevant elements of the right size as is critical to the project goal and treat everything else as overproduction waste. This is easier said than done. For example, if we wish to fix an imperfect interface between a patient monitoring device in an ICU and the nurses monitoring the device, and the nurses' competence in the device use is not questioned, we would probably look at the device outputs, alarms, connections, and perhaps at the technician(s) who installed and maintained the device. We would certainly ignore the long list of folks who designed and manufactured the device, who work in the device supply chain, who wrote the regulations which were the basis for creating and using the device, etc. But if the problem persists for many such devices in a given ICU (but not in ICUs in other hospitals where the same device is used), we should probably include the stakeholders involved in training the technicians, and those who train the nurses in the device usage. Indeed, problem context, common sense, experience, even tribal knowledge are all useful when selecting N. Also, we should have open minds for possible alternative solutions, approaches, and experiments. It is critical to start by talking to the local stakeholders, hearing and understanding their frustrations, and performing Gemba walks. When selecting the right N, iterations are common: we start with some N elements, then discover that we missed one or more of the important ones, or that some are irrelevant, and alter the number.

Consider the evil of fragmentation in a routine case of a patient seeing a Primary Care Provider (PCP) with a complaint of a persistent moderate pain in the belly cavity. Before making a final diagnosis, the doctor begins by ordering blood work. A local phlebotomist prepares the labels, draws blood samples into a few vials, attaches the labels, and sends them to a nearby clinical laboratory. The samples are transported to the lab, sorted with numerous other samples, analyzed, resulted, and the result is automatically sent back to the ordering physician using Electronic Health Records (EHR). This appears to be a simple, totally routine case involving the following elements in our SoI: patient, physician, physician's nurse, phlebotomist, and clinical lab. (In this example, for the sake of simplicity, we use a shortened list of stakeholders, ignoring clinic scheduler, receptionist and nurses, lab equipment maintenance technicians, equipment engineers and manufacturers, data entry clerk in the labs, transport driver(s), billing clerks, and hundreds of others.) Once we have the five main system elements identified (N = 5), we can construct the N^2 matrix, where we list the elements as both rows and columns, as shown in Figure 2.2. Ignoring the cells on the main diagonal, the remaining N(N-1) cells (20 in this example) show a possible interface or interaction (bi-directional or symmetric) between any pair of the elements. **Each cell represents an opportunity for the shown interface to go wrong**. To dig deeper into our example, consider the interaction between the ordering PCP and the clinical laboratory performing the test, indicated in Figure 2.2 with arrows.

	Patient	PCP	Nurse	Phlebotomist	Clinical Lab
Patient					
PCP					
Nurse					
Phlebotomist					
Clinical Lab					

Figure 2.2   The N^2 Matrix for a Routine Medical Visit.

What can go wrong in this simple, routine interaction between the PCP and the lab? Here is a short list:

a. The PCP's nurse may have been too distracted to hand the written order for the lab to the patient before the patient left the clinic.
b. The patient received the order but may have failed to see the phlebotomist to give blood (rushing to work or to small children at home …)
c. The overworked phlebotomist may have placed the blood samples in the wrong containers (for different test types the samples need to be mixed with different chemicals in designated vials).
d. A sample may have been dropped on the floor somewhere near the phlebotomy station and rolled out of sight.
e. A sample may have been lost in the clinical laboratory.
f. The sample was analyzed but the system failed to result it (perhaps a momentary power loss in the interface between the analyzing instrument and the receiving computer).
g. The sample was resulted, but the system failed to send notification to the ordering PCP. Perhaps the PCP is a new employee for whom the EHR connection has not yet been fully activated.
h. And the worst: the test was positive, the PCP received the result, and failed to follow up with the patient. Undiagnosed patient went into a coma.

Each of the above events has low but not zero probability[4], and each has potentially fatal consequences if ignored especially if the test were positive for a serious disease. The above scenarios are notional only, to illustrate our approach. In reality, many more people are involved in each step, and there are many more opportunities for things to go wrong, but those discussed probably cover the main fragmentation problems. In our example, systems engineers would then proceed to specify requirements to fix the system so

Table 2.1 Issues and the Goals[5] to Fix Problems (a)–(g)

Issue in PCP-Lab Interaction	Goal to Fix Issue
a. The nurse may have forgotten to hand the written order for labs to the patient.	Nurses shall be given a special tray for the orders, to be checked before each patient leaves.
b. The patient may have failed to see the phlebotomist to give blood.	The system shall be modified to issue automatic reminders to the patient by text, email, and robocall. If not successful, a live phone call shall be made.
c. The phlebotomist may have placed the blood sample in the wrong container.	Phlebotomy station shall be reorganized with color posters and sorting trays to visibly indicate the right containers to use, followed by training of phlebotomists.
d. The sample may have been lost at the phlebotomy station.	The system shall be modified to raise alarm and ask the patient by text, email, and robocall to revisit phlebotomy. If not successful, a live phone call shall be made.
e. The sample was lost in the lab.	Same as (d).
f. The sample was analyzed, but the system failed to result it.	The system shall recognize the lack of result and will analyze the spare sample, if available, or (d).
g. The sample was resulted, but the system failed to notify the ordering PCP.	The EHR shall issue alarm to the PCP after waiting for 5 days.

that the fragmentation events (a-h) would be mitigated, reacting to the events with corrective actions, preventing the events from occurring, or lowering the probability of occurrence. The right column of Table 2.1 illustrates the possible project goals needed to fix the above interfaces. The fixes are a matter of common sense and experience.

The goals would serve to implement the indicated corrective actions as a project. This is a classic example of healthcare fragmentation and the power of LHSE in identifying fragmented pieces. The steps demonstrated in Figures 2.2 and Table 2.1 should be repeated for all applicable interface cells in the N^2 matrix.

Routine healthcare operations typically do not involve that level of fragmentation details until and unless a dramatic need arises, such as patient mortality, a legal case, or competitive pressure. At this point, managers realize that the existing fragmentation is unacceptable and must be addressed. As demonstrated, LHSE contributes a high level of logical rigor into the process of dealing with the fragmentation. Notice that no mathematics or hard-core

---

BOX 2.2   STEPS IN N^2 MATRIX AND INTERFACE ANALYSIS

I. Create the N^2 matrix listing relevant system elements (stakeholders and other nodes) as both rows and columns
II. Shade the cells on the main diagonal having no interfaces with themselves
III. Denote other cells using some convenient unique letter code showing the present interface means, for example:

D = "dropped ball" or no communication
E = communication to/from/via EHR
H = huddle
F = face-to-face consultation
P = phone
M = email
C = postal card
R = "routine step"
Etc.

IV. Show in colors the broken interactions (red), problematic (yellow), and those working well (green). (The example in Figure 2.2 does not show the color markings yet.)
V. Later, when we present the project solution, we may repeat the matrix showing improved interfaces, hopefully all in green color.
VI. In each interface that is less than perfect (red or yellow), the team should use local knowledge and expertise to list all items that can go wrong in the given interface (such as the events a-h in the first column of Table 2.1). When identifying problems, it is critical to involve stakeholders from both sides of the interface. The problem items (a–h) will be used later for formulating corrective action goals and, subsequently, requirements.

engineering were used. The key step was to identify all elements in our SoI. Having identified these elements, the interfaces and goals follow logically. Box 2.2 summarizes the steps of creating the N^2 matrix and formulating the goals.

The reader is invited to compare the rigor of this approach to the traditional approach, where only those interfaces which created some kind of a visible trouble would be identified and acted upon: patient harm, a legal or disciplinary action, or such. Others tend to remain in hiding. The LHSE provides rigorous identification of all interfaces[6].

Recall the relatively small problem size of our fragmentation example of a patient seeing a doctor with a belly pain complaint. In this medically routine example, we identified N = 5 system elements, resulting in N(N − 1) = 20 active interfaces, each having several potential fragmentation issues. In the cell analyzed, we found 8 problems (a–h). If all other active cells would also present 8 problems, we would have 20 × 8 = 160 fragmentation problems to address. This would be a medium-size healthcare project. Dear reader: do not panic at this point. All such fragmentation problems tend to be mitigated with only a few common modifications of the informatics, or procedures. Also, most projects dealing with healthcare delivery improvements involve only a few problems, often only one (e.g., reduce room turnover time in hospital; or reduce patient discharge time from hospital). Additional simplifications can be achieved by noticing that in many workflows, not all stakeholders interact with each other at the same time. Usually, they interact in smaller subgroups. Thus, we can reduce the problem size by considering two or more groups of stakeholders and their corresponding N^2 matrices. In the above PCP-laboratory example, one group may involve the patient, nurse and phlebotomist, and the other the patient, PCP and the laboratory, each yielding a 3 × 3 matrix with 3 × 2 = 6 active cells, for a total of 12 active cells rather than one 5 × 4 = 20 active cells.

2.2.3 Architecting the Current State; DODAF Charts, Process Map, Current State VSM

According to the adage "a picture is worth a thousand words," the usefulness of good graphical representations of systems and work processes cannot be overstated. In systems engineering we use architecting charts for that purpose.

Most of architecting charts are useful in the next phase of the LHSE project, Design of Future State. This is where we architect our solution. Some charts are also useful in the AoCS, as follows.

Process charts and Lean value stream maps are useful architecting means, quite popular in healthcare. The Process Map, or if the data on waste is available, the Current State Value Stream Map (CS VSM) are used to illustrate the current workflow. The CS VSM is like a process map but with added information about wastes and timing measured at different workflow points. Recall that in Lean we define eight waste types: overproduction, inventory, waiting, over processing, motion, transportation, defects, and waste of human potential [Oppenheim, 2011]. In healthcare applications, we rarely have the luxury of time and budget to measure all eight accurately. Everyone working in healthcare understands that the dominant category of waste is waiting: patients waiting for activities, activities waiting for patients, providers waiting for other providers or information, nurses waiting for doctors, etc. So, just focusing on waiting waste alone usually leads to vast improvements. But other wastes may be important too. Patient safety is focused on avoidance of defects because in healthcare they can have deadly consequences. Poorly architected clinic and hospital spaces can yield motion and transportation waste, which is easy to analyze using the so-called spaghetti and time charts. Poorly designed, especially bureaucratic tasks and processes can yield overproduction and overprocessing waste. Poorly managed inventories of supplies and medicines can yield inventory waste, and poorly scheduled medical activities can yield patient batching which transforms into the waiting and human-inventory waste. And the waste of human potential manifests itself in the form of provider's burnout, an increasingly critical characteristic of healthcare work. So, there is a lot of information that can be captured and shown on the CS VSM. Once this map is available, the Design of Future State will be so much easier to create, and much more effective. But if data on waste and timing is not available, or not relevant to the project, a Process Map alone should be used. Figures 2.3 and 2.4 illustrate a sample process map and a sample CS VSM. The timing of various activities shown at the bottom of the process map is useful, if available.

At the risk of restating the well-known practice of drawing VSM, we recommend:

- Marking all tasks on the VSM in one of the following colors: VA in green, NVA in red, and RNVA in yellow.
- When showing the Future State VSM (FS VSM), show the CS VSM in small scale somewhere in a blank area of the FS VSM chart for easy visual identification of the eliminated "red and yellow" tasks.
- Show particularly nasty problems and frustrations with a burst symbol and brief descriptions.
- If the map is simple, we can enter the waste information directly on it.

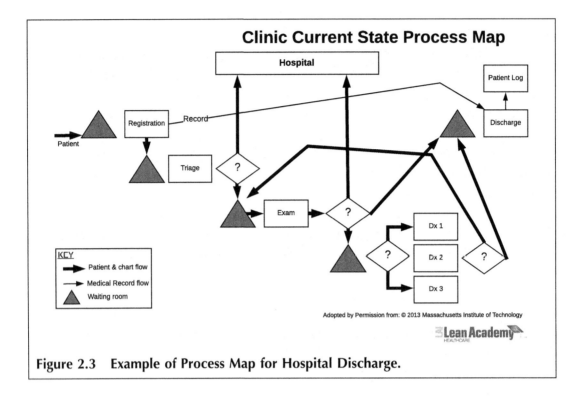

Figure 2.3   Example of Process Map for Hospital Discharge.

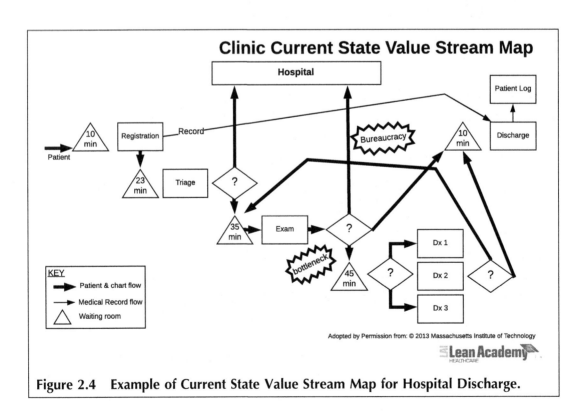

Figure 2.4   Example of Current State Value Stream Map for Hospital Discharge.

Otherwise, we number the activity boxes sequentially and show a separate table listing and explaining the waste values.

■ If the project uses Lean methodology, both CS VSM and FS VSM should
be included.

The most comprehensive set of system architecting views is defined in the
Department of Defense Architectural Framework (DODAF) [DODAF, 2009].
DODAF specifies 25 different views showing the system structure, interacting
nodes, interfaces, information flows, data flows, and many others. We use as
many views as we need to illustrate what we think should be illustrated and
no more. In typical healthcare projects we only need a few, even only one. At
the risk of displeasure of DODAF purists, this author believes that it is perfectly acceptable to combine more than one view on a single chart. For example, Figure 2.1 shown earlier can be regarded as an SoI architecting view.
More examples will be shown in Section 2.3.7.

For completeness of listing architecting views, we mention the Sources-
Inputs-Process-Outputs-Customers (SIPOC) diagrams, but they usually only
make sense in the Design of Future State, and examples will be provided in
Section 2.3.7. The Current State is often so messy that drawing an orderly
SIPOC would be impractical.

2.2.4 *Fishbone Diagram to Analyze Problem Causes*

The Ishikawa (also called Fishbone) diagram [Wedgewood, 2007] is a simple but
powerful tool which illustrates the potentially causal factors for a particular
outcome or problem. It visually organizes various causes of the problem into
logical groupings and illustrates them in an easy to understand graph. Figure 2.5
illustrates the example of an exceedingly slow patient discharge from a hospital.
The problem (slow discharge, shown as DPT > 2 Hours) is shown in the
rightmost box, often illustrated as a fish head, thus the name. The "bones" or
"branches" of the diagram list the possible causes. The main branches are frequently labeled "people or personnel," "equipment or technology," "processes
or methods," "environment or social factors," and "materials," if relevant. These
categories are not "set in stone" so other names that are better suited to the SoI
can be used. Sub-branches are added as applicable, as shown in Figure 2.5.

The Ischikawa diagram is taken from a menu of Six Sigma tools
[Wedgewood, 2007]. The author finds it particularly useful for analyzing
causes of problems, but other Six Sigma tools such as the Pareto diagram,
scatter diagram, control charts, regression, spaghetti chart, time chart, and any

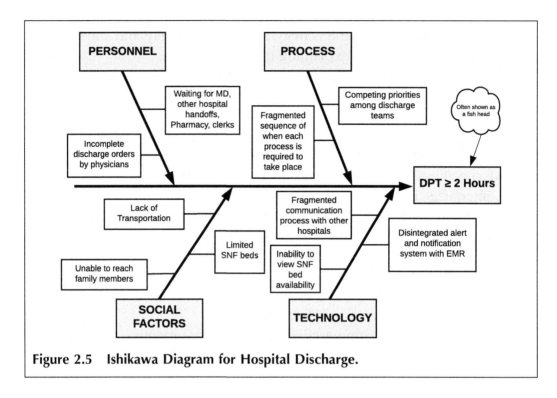

Figure 2.5   Ishikawa Diagram for Hospital Discharge.

other from the rich menu of quality and failure analysis tools can be used. Healthcare is a vast domain and each problem may require distinct tools. The decision as to which tools to use in the AoCS should be governed by the bottom line: we seek solid, truthful, objective, complete, and sufficiently granular evidence and understanding of the current state.

2.2.5 Problem Statement

The Problem Statement should be the last element of the AoCS[7]. It is the culmination point or "big bang" of the AoCS. At this step, we must have a perfect, complete, clear, unambiguous, qualitative, and quantitative understanding of the system of interest, its problems, wastes, fragmentation, frustrations, miscommunications, etc.

The Problem Statement is a brief statement precisely summarizing the problem to be addressed in the project. It is a critical element in the LHSE process rigor because it will drive all subsequent project steps in the Design of Future State, described in Section 2.3. A poorly formulated Problem Statement almost guarantees imperfect project outcome.

When formulating the Problem Statement, we should be inspired by Lean thinking: let us not try to solve "the whole healthcare universe." Let us not list everything that is wrong in our institution; and in healthcare any halfwit can list tons of frustrations, grievances, and problems. Let us be realistic and focus on a specific problem or set of related problems that will lead to realistic feasible solutions. The Problem Statement should be limited to stating the problem. It should be "solution agnostic," that is, not attempt to present or suggest any solution.

The following is an example of a good Problem Statement:

> **PROJECT PROBLEM STATEMENT**
> **In hospital X the average discharge time of patients from the hospital is 24 hours, while other hospitals with similar patient demographics and locations average under two hours. The excessive time is attributed to (1) inefficient interactions with outside stakeholders (insurance, SNFs, hospices, boarding facilities, outside transportation, family, DME vendors, and other hospitals) as well as (2) imperfect proactive planning, coordination, and lack of concurrency in the discharge process steps.**

Formulating the Problem Statement at the end of the AoCS assures a mature informed statement. Some healthcare projects state the problem at the beginning, in the Background section. For example, an excessive discharge time from the hospital is a problem that is usually well known to stakeholders even before the project is started and authorized, so there is a natural temptation to state it right at the beginning of the project. But the LHSE rigor requires that in the Background section we just state it as perhaps a "project objective," for example, "reduce excessive discharge time," but do not attempt to be too precise before we have a chance to analyze the problem at depth. Doing so assures that we do not "jump the gun" and enables us to formulate a well-informed Problem Statement.

2.3 Design of Future State (DoFS)

In the Analysis of Current State, besides healthcare and systems engineering, we used tools from a mixed bag of other knowledge domains: Lean Six Sigma, project management; perhaps also medicine, IT, engineering, and law. In contrast, the steps used in the Design of Future State (DoFS) match selected tools of systems engineering quite closely.

2.3.1 Goal Statement

We ended the AoCS with a well-informed Problem Statement. We begin the DoFS with a Goal Statement. The Goal Statement should be a mirror image of the Problem Statement, just changing "what is wrong" to "what we need to do to fix it." It should be a concise statement on what this project is to accomplish. It should be formulated with the same clarity as the Problem Statement.

As discussed in the last section, the Goal should be realistic and feasible, otherwise we may doom the project to fail. The Goal is different from a requirement; it is only meant as a starting point to formulate the corresponding quantitative and verifiable requirement(s). The Goal represents the project objective but does not include the legal details that would make it verifiable in a binary way of pass/fail. Goals are to be validated in the last step of the DoFS. In other words, we follow this rule:

- Requirements must be verified (more on this later)
- Goals must be validated

The number of Goals should be small, often only one; having too many goals risks prolonged iterations and conflicts among stakeholders. It is better to split a project with too many goals into several smaller projects each with only one or a few goals. The following is an example of a Goal Statement (compare it to the Problem Statement):

PROJECT GOAL STATEMENT
Improve the average discharge time of patients from hospital X to be competitive with other hospitals in the location, consistently under two hours, by redesigning:

1. **interactions with outside stakeholders (insurance, SNFs, hospices, boarding facilities, outside transportation, family, DME vendors, and other hospitals), as well as**
2. **internal activities, including proactive planning, coordination, and concurrency in the discharge process steps.**

Notice that the Goal statement lacks the verifiable details; that is intentional. The details are provided in Requirements.

2.3.2 Requirements

Rigorous formulation of project requirements is a critical step of LHSE. Requirements interpret Goals into precise characteristics of the desired Future State. In several places, this book has emphasized a high level of logical rigor provided by the LHSE process. Specifically, LHSE provides the rigor as follows:

- The Problem Statement is informed by a comprehensive Analysis of Current State
- The Goal Statement is a "mirror image" of the Problem Statement informing what this project is to achieve
- The Goal Statement leads to a precise and verifiable Requirement statement.

This sequence of rigorous logical steps of Problem-Goal-Requirements contributes to a high probability of successful outcome.

For success, we must have objective means of stating what is required and then verifying that it was in fact accomplished. Projects are often executed by a team of people other than the users of the project results. In such cases, there may be a potential conflict between the two groups. The project team may claim that they did what they understood was expected, and the users may claim that what was done was not good enough for their needs. Precise and verifiable requirements are the rigorous tools needed to prevent such conflict and leave no "wiggle room" to either side.

Requirements should be achievable but solution agnostic. In other words, when writing a requirement, we should not be constrained by how we might implement it. Concerns regarding implementation will be handled in the subsequent risk analysis. However, requirements must be achievable; it would be counterproductive to write a requirement that we know *a priori* to be impossible to achieve.

Each requirement must be objectively verifiable. This implies that each requirement must be written with sufficient precision, clarity, lack of ambiguity and single meaning, so that every stakeholder will understand it in the same manner, and that the verification can only be binary: pass/fail. Each requirement must have the word "shall" in it, as in "… the patient discharge time shall be reduced to …." We should not combine several different aspects into a single requirement because verification may then be difficult, confusing as to which aspect is being verified and to what degree. Box 2.3 illustrates a bad requirement, the reasons why it is poorly written, and a corrected, verifiable requirement.

BOX 2.3   EXAMPLE OF A BAD AND GOOD REQUIREMENT

Bad requirement:

The discharge time from hospital X and from the hospital ED will be reduced to be below the value of competitive hospitals.

Why is this a bad requirement?

- Not verifiable, ambiguous, unclear.
- Lacking the word "shall"
- Convoluting two different discharges: from hospital and from ED.
- Not clear how the time is to be measured. As average? And if so, measured over what period? As a maximum? And measured during what period?
- What is the value being compared to? Which other hospitals are being considered?
- By what date is this to be accomplished?

Good requirement:

The average discharge time of all patients from hospital X measured over a 30-day period starting on [specific date] shall be reduced to under two hours. The discharge time to be measured from the time of issuing discharge orders by the attending MD to the moment when the patient is wheeled outside of the hospital building. The reduction shall be demonstrated by [specific date].

Each requirement shall be accompanied by a specification of how it will be verified. Verification must be done by one of the four following methods: test, measurement, inspection, or analysis [Walden, 2015].

It is a good practice to organize the requirements and their verifications into a table with the following columns:

- Requirement sequential number 1, 2, 3 etc. Some top-level requirements may have lower-level or derived requirements. Then, we need to keep track of parent-child relationships, and number the lower-level requirements 1.1, 1.2, etc.
- Requirement text.
- Requirement "owner" (the stakeholder who included this requirement), and/or justification for the requirement. The stakeholder should be a person's name and phone number rather than a department or organization name, for easy locating of the person in case of questions.
- Verification means (test, measurement, inspection, or analysis).

Table 2.2 presents the Requirement table template.

Table 2.2 Requirements Table

#	Requirement text	Owner / Justification	Verification means
1			
2			
3			
Etc.			

In healthcare delivery projects, the number of requirements is typically small: one to a few. A larger number (measured in tens) can result from the interface analysis such as that shown in Table 2.1. In this case, some requirements will "fall out" from the mitigation goals, such as those listed in the last column of Table 2.1. These goals would be interpreted into requirements shown in Table 2.3. The owner column lists "system" as the owner. We make that entry when the entire system needs the requirement.

Table 2.3 Requirements to Achieve the Goals of Table 2.1

#	Requirement text	Owner / Justification	Verification means
1	The IT system shall recognize when the patient failed to give a blood sample within one week of the provider's order.	Systems	Inspection
2	When the patient failed to give a blood sample, the IT system shall contact the patient repeatedly once a day using [agreed communications means] until the sample is received.	Systems	Inspection
3	The system shall track the sample until the result is entered into EHR within [prescribed amount of time].	Systems	Inspection
4	If the sample is lost and not found in [the prescribed amount of time], the system shall contact the patient repeatedly once a day using [agreed communications means] until another sample is provided.	Systems	Inspection
5	A positive test result shall be flagged in red color on the EHR screen of the ordering provider.	Systems	Inspection
6	A positive test result shall be acknowledged in EHR by the ordering provider.	Systems	Inspection

Box 2.4 lists six types of requirements listed in INCOSE Handbook [Walden et al., 2015]. In healthcare delivery projects, the most common types seem to be 3, 2, 5, in this order, based on anecdotal knowledge.

BOX 2.4 DIFFERENT TYPES OF REQUIREMENTS

1. **Business requirements.** These include high-level statements of goals, objectives, and needs of the enterprise.
2. **Stakeholder requirements.** The needs of discrete stakeholder groups are also specified to define what they expect from a particular solution.
3. **Solution requirements.** Solution requirements describe the characteristics that a system/product must have to meet the needs of the stakeholders and the business itself.
4. **Nonfunctional** requirements describe the general characteristics of a system. They are also known as *quality attributes*.
5. **Functional** requirements describe how a product must behave, its features, and functions. **A functional requirement describes *what* a system should do, while non-functional requirements place constraints on *how* the system will do so.**
6. **Transition requirements.** An additional group of requirements defines what is needed from an organization to successfully move from its current state to its desired state with the new product.

2.3.3 Project Interrogatives

If the project involves a team of people, it might be useful to borrow a tool from the project management domain, called Project Interrogatives [Spewak, 1992]. It is a set of six questions symbolically described as "who, what, where, when, why, and how" – which, when answered, make it clear how the project execution responsibilities are distributed:

- Who: who is to do it?
- What: what action is to be done or is needed?
- Where: where is it to be done or needed?
- When: when is it to be done or needed?

- Why: why is it to be done or needed?
- How: how is it to be done?

This information injects clarity into the project execution. This step of LHSE is optional and should be left to the project manager to decide whether to use it or not. Very small teams (1–2 people) probably do not need it. Similar interrogatives may also be used in the project Implementation phase, as the individuals implementing the project results may be different than those executing the project.

The Appendix presents an interesting alternative proposed for medical care systems by the UK Royal Academy of Engineering [Royal Academy, 2017]. It is a set of questions much more comprehensive than the above interrogatories. In the opinion of the present author, it might be a preferred approach for much larger healthcare systems than those discussed in this book.

2.3.4 ConOps (Concept of Operations)

A concept of operations (abbreviated **CONOPS** or **ConOps**) is a document describing the intended use or operations of the system. It may include verbal descriptions how the SoI should be used, by whom, when, under what circumstances, subject to what limitations; what training will be required to use it, etc. [Walden et al., 2015]. ConOps are formulated as informative rather than imperative sentences. They are less formal than requirements. Box 2.5 presents a ConOps example.

BOX 2.5 CONOPS EXAMPLE

ConOps Example

The form with patient data to be printed from the Electronic Health Records (EHR) will be used by Residents for the subsequent morning rounds in the hospital Burn Unit. The form will be printed during the 6:50–7:00 AM time block for morning rounds that start at 8 AM. The Residents will use the one-hour time gap of 7:00–8:00 AM to study the printed patient data and be ready to present it to the medical team making the rounds. The new electronic module of EHR will automatically extract and print all specified data on the form, one page per patient; a Resident will only need to enter the patients' IDs. The data to be printed and the form format are defined in Requirement No. x.

2.3.5 *Analysis of Alternatives*

Once the requirements are defined, we can proceed to the solution creation. It is critically important not to "jump to a conclusion," selecting a particular solution[8] right away without first considering all reasonable solution alternatives. The Analysis of Alternatives (AoA) is an important step of LHSE, used to identify the solution candidates, agree on the means to evaluate them objectively, and select the best one. Recall that requirements are supposed to be solution agnostic.

The AoA includes the following steps: identification of candidate solutions, selection of measures of effectiveness, and the candidate selection. They are discussed next.

Identification of Candidate Solution Alternatives. We first select candidate solutions and subject them to analysis. Among the candidates we should always include "do nothing," in other words, keep the current state. Including it as an alternative will enable us to compare other proposed candidates to the current state using the same measures. Typically, in healthcare projects, we identify 2–4 candidate solutions (in addition to "do nothing"), all of which appear reasonable and have a good chance to satisfy the requirements. Typically, the candidates are proposed by stakeholders of the system, based on their experience, creativity, and benchmarking with competition, as well as solid understanding of the requirements. It is important to allow junior team members to propose their candidates and not to permit the authority gradient to stifle creativity. Surely, experience plays an important role, however, junior members' creativity is often invaluable, especially when we are dealing with modern technologies, IT, electronics, etc.

As an example, consider three Alternatives for the patient discharge from the hospital:

Alternative 1: Do Nothing (keep the current state). The patients remain in their hospital bed until destination is assured and transportation is ready and waiting.

Alternative 2: Discharge Lounge. A new discharge lounge will be organized. Soon after the discharge orders, the patients would be wheeled to the lounge, either in their hospital beds, with the lounge spaces separated from other patients by soft curtains, or in a wheelchair, in a common area. Standard discharge activities, such as payments, printing of discharge orders, delivery of medicines, ordering of durable equipment, and communications with family or nursing facilities, would be conducted while the patient is waiting in the lounge. The lounge would be staffed by two individuals: a lounge clerk and a medical nurse. When the patient is wheeled to the lounge, the hospital room left by the patient can be immediately cleaned, sanitized, and restocked and made available to the next hospital patient.

Alternative 3: Waiting Room. There is no discharge lounge, just a simple waiting room. Patients that need to use a hospital bed would remain in the hospital bed until discharged (i.e., like Alternative 1), and patients that can be moved in wheelchairs and need no medical care would be moved to the discharge waiting room. The waiting room would not have any attending nurse, just a clerk who handles payments, printing of discharge orders, delivery of medicines, ordering of durable equipment, and communications with the destination. It is estimated that 75% of the patients could be in this group.

Measures of Effectiveness (MoE). After selecting the candidate solutions, the next step of the AoA is to specify MoE that we will apply to rank and judge candidate solutions as objectively as possible. Typical MoE are safety, cost, level of effort, turnaround time, wait time, ease of use, time to implement, patient acceptance, stakeholder acceptance, perhaps union acceptance, and others, but not all of them need to be applied in a given AoA. We should be driven here by common sense and experience, as well as Lean Thinking ("do what is needed and no more"). A common practice is to use ranking scales for the MoEs, typically 1–5, with 1 being the least attractive and 5 being the most attractive, but other scales can be used if desired (for example, the Pugh scale of −2, −1, 0, 1 and 2 is popular, with −2 the least and 2 the most attractive). The allocation of particular values to different alternatives is, of necessity, somewhat arbitrary. It is an "educated guess," a judgment call. Experience in the project domain is invaluable here. The exact value is not critical if the relative rankings are correct. AoA in healthcare delivery projects is not meant to be a huge effort, consuming precious project budget and schedule. Educated guesses are usually "good enough." Performing detailed quantitative analysis of the measures appears to be an overkill and contradicts the Lean approach. Usually, it is fairly evident what measure value we should assign a given candidate alternative.

In the example of patient discharge from the hospital, let us use the following MoEs:

■ Patient safety
■ Patient comfort

- Cost of stay in the Lounge
- Hospital bed utilization

Candidate Selection. Continuing with our example, now we can apply the selected MoEs to the three alternatives, as shown in Table 2.4.

Table 2.4 Analysis of Alternatives

Description of Alternative ⟶	Alternative 1	Alternative 2	Alternative 3
MoE			
Cost of stay in the lounge	1	5	1
Patient safety	5	4	4
Patient comfort	5	4	3
Hospital bed utilization	1	5	4
SUMS	12	18	12

The example is for illustration only and is not to imply any recommended solution.

The last row in Table 2.4 contains the sum of the ranking values. In this case, the Discharge Lounge, with the sum value of 18 is the winning alternative. This winner now becomes the subject of the subsequent steps of the LHSE process.

If we could estimate the actual non-recurring cost of constructing the Discharge Lounge plus the operating costs, and compare them to the cost of discharged patients occupying hospital beds, we could perform a formal business case for or against the Discharge Lounge. This is outside the scope of the current book.

Even though we use educated guesses rather than science-based values on the ranking scales, the rigor of the AoA process is higher than an arbitrary decision up front to use only one solution idea.

2.3.6 *Design of Future State*

Once we select a single alternative, we can proceed to a detailed design of the SoI future state, as shown in Figure 1.4. Normally, this step represents the major effort of the project. The step is often iterative: we start with a design of the selected alternative, architect it (Section 2.3.7), and iterate it until we acquire certainty that all requirements can be verified, and all project goals validated.

The knowledge utilized in this step is the healthcare, medical, IT, engineering or legal knowledge of the project subject rather than LHSE. The LHSE process provides the necessary rigorous inputs into the design (goals, requirements, ConOps, and AoA), and will use the design outputs to rigorously architect, analyze for risks, verify, validate, and implement the designed SoI. These steps of LHSE are explained in the subsequent sections of the book. But the design itself is specific to a given clinical environment of the SoI, so we leave this step to healthcare and medical experts among the project stakeholders.

In some projects that start small but are intended to be expandable and scalable, modularity is a critical characteristic. For example, the seminal paper by [Kanter et al., 2013] describes the Complete Care project at Kaiser Permanente, which addresses treatments for 26 wellness and chronic medical conditions. The project started small for only a few medical conditions but created a general framework and common electronic and logical modules and dissemination means, which were gradually expanded to other medical conditions and applied throughout the Southern California Kaiser Permanente system.

2.3.7 *System Architecting*

In healthcare delivery projects, "design of an SoI" usually involves a redesign or a new design of a workflow or care. The architecting step of LHSE is often a part of the design process described in Section 2.3.6 rather than just an illustration of the final solution. We brainstorm the best possible design that, we hope, will satisfy the requirements and architect it, and the architecting provides efficient visual and logical feedback to the design, which then can be improved, and so on.

The role of the architecting views or charts is to graphically present in an easy-to-understand way, the relevant information about the system elements, workflows, and interfaces, including the flow of information "from-to." The graphs are there to help us understand the design, to improve it, explain it to stakeholders, and avoid miscommunications. The most common architecting views used in healthcare delivery projects are as follows.

■ **Future State Value Stream Map (FS VSM)**
  Future State Value Stream Map (FS VSM) is a "twin brother" to the Current State VSM if we use Lean methodology in the project. FS VSM presents the streamlined process from which we eliminated wastes. The FS VSM is a powerful tool for streamlining processes, but it is not effective in il-lustrating information flow between the steps, particularly the informa-tion fragmentation. Therefore, in addition to Lean, we need to use the

LHSE including architecting tools. Graphically, FS VSM looks like the CS VSM, but, if we did the waste elimination from Current State properly, it should be simpler and cleaner looking than the CS VSM. Value Stream Mapping is beyond the scope of this book. The reader is referred to [Graban, 2012; Jimmerson, 2010].

■ DODAF Views

DODAF views, already introduced in Section 2.2.3, are highly useful in illustrating design architecture. The most common in healthcare projects are Operational View 1 (OV1), Systems View 1 (SV1), and Data Flow View 1 (DF1), [Walden et al., 2015]. SV1 shows hardware subsystems and interfaces, as illustrated in Figure 2.6. OV1 shows high-level tasks and activities. DF1 is convenient for illustrating high-level data flows between system elements.

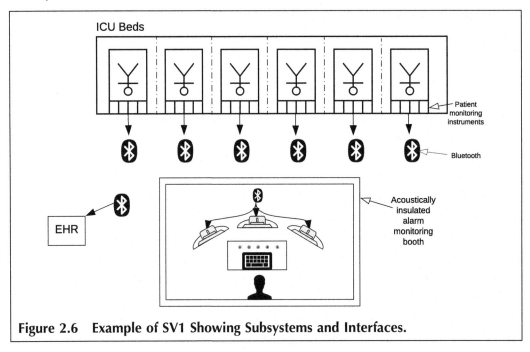

Figure 2.6   Example of SV1 Showing Subsystems and Interfaces.

Nothing prevents us from combining different standard DODAF views, if doing so makes sense[9]. Figure 2.7 illustrates such a combined OV1/DF1 view for our hospital discharge problem. Here, we show the subsystems, activities, and information flows between them, including negotiations among the parties. The symbols and connections are not formally defined and can be made up as we go along. Many graphics software is commercially available for drawing architecting views.

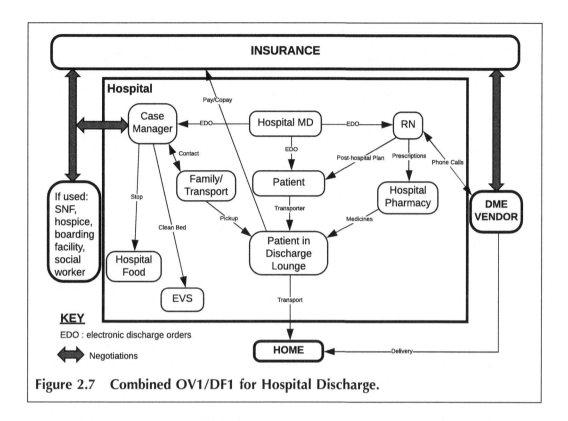

Figure 2.7   Combined OV1/DF1 for Hospital Discharge.

■ **Source-Inputs-Process-Outputs-Customers (SIPOC) Diagrams**

SIPOC diagram is of special importance in fragmented healthcare operations. It is ideal for precise illustration of inputs and outputs of a given activity (process or task). The diagram shows the input information flows from sources to the process of interest, as well as the output data created by the process and the customers or destinations where the outputs are sent. Each diagram must describe only a single process, task, or activity. Inputs and outputs are information. Sources and destinations can be individual human beings, organizational nodes (e.g., clinical laboratory), departments, or EHR. If the process is subject to an approval or "signature" of a supervisor, we indicate that activity by a control box in the diagram.

SIPOCs have proven themselves in the common situations where a provider (often a nurse or a hospital administrator) must repeatedly interact with different stakeholders, receiving information (inputs) from some of them (sources), processing the information (process), and sending the outputs to other stakeholders (customers or destinations). A generic SIPOC is shown in Figure 2.8.

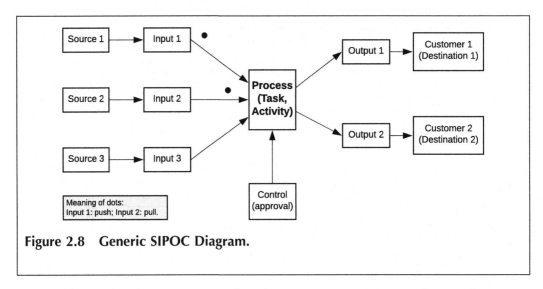

Figure 2.8 Generic SIPOC Diagram.

Additional information may be shown in a SIPOC specifying who is responsible for the information transmission: whether it is the input source pushing the information to the process, or the process pulling the information from the source. For example, we can show who is responsible for sending the information between the process and its destination, whether the process is pushing it or the customer is pulling it. This can be easily indicated in the SIPOC with a simple dot at the proper end of the arrow.

A given source may create more than one input. More than one output may go to a given destination. Any number of inputs, sources, outputs, and destinations may be shown in a single SIPOC, but there must be only one process per SIPOC. Figure 2.9 illustrates a SIPOC example for the hospital discharge process conducted by a Discharge Nurse. The nurse receives patient discharge orders (inputs) from the attending MD, and creates several outputs that go to the patient, a DME vendor, pharmacy, transporters, and EHR. The work of the Discharge Nurse is supervised by the Charge Nurse (for simplicity, we omitted destinations of SNFs and other continued care facilities).

SIPOCs have demonstrated their exceptional utility in the fragmented healthcare processes in which a stakeholder, typically the MD in charge of the patient or his/her RN, or Nurse Coordinator (often called nurse navigator), or an administrator repeatedly has to be in contact with a number of stakeholders for a large number of patients. The author has seen clinic and hospital organizations, where the lack of SIPOCs caused significant chaos, delays,

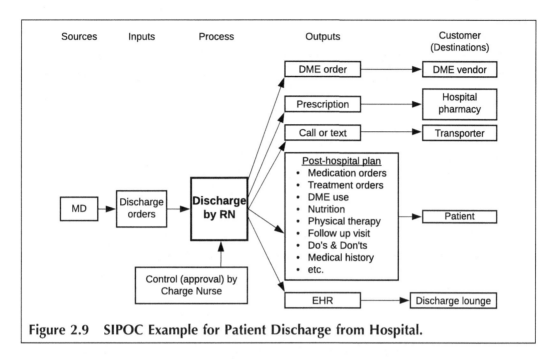

Figure 2.9 SIPOC Example for Patient Discharge from Hospital.

"dropped balls," frustrations, provider burnout, and patient safety risks. A simple SIPOC tends to "clean" the activities, making it self-evident what information is expected and who is to provide or request it.

SIPOCs can be shown in a series of subsequent processes, or as a network, where an output from one serves as an input to another. However, it is critical to separate the different SIPOCs from each other and not show them comingled together, as this only causes confusion. Let us repeat again: **each SIPOC shows only one Process**.

An excellent example of the SIPOC application was the UCLA Health project of integrating a highly fragmented Adolescent and Young Adult (AYA) cancer treatment process. The process involves many activities: cancer treatment, mental health, social support, financial support, clinical trials, fertility preservations, and others for thousands of young, frightened, and confused patients. Thousands of such patients are treated yearly. S. Speicher, MD, integrated the system using (1) a nurse navigator, who used (2) a modified EHR system, which followed (3) several well defined SIPOC processes. [https://sean-story.wistia.com/medias/bs62oygize].

2.3.8 Risk and Opportunity Management

At its simplest, Risk Management proactively identifies "what might go wrong" with the system design and prevents it. Risk is a potential problem or threat that could affect the project ability to deliver satisfactory SoI, meet its performance, cost, schedule, or other objectives [Lockheed Martin, 2020]. Proactivity, the mantra of good management, assures that we will not be surprised by bad outcomes and will have enough time to prevent them or to mitigate them **before they occur**. The alternative to risk management is to do nothing, a reactive management, also called crisis management, where we allow adverse events to occur and only then try corrective actions, if not too late and if possible. And adverse events are usually not static: they tend to expand to crisis proportions; one problem generates others, etc. Popular heuristic indicates that reactive management requires dramatically more resources, higher level of expertise to deal with the resultant crisis, and causes delays, budget overruns, and frustrations for all involved.

In the context of risk, we can classify decision-making into three knowledge categories: complete uncertainty, relative uncertainty, and complete certainty. In complete uncertainty, we are dealing with "unknown unknowns," that is, we do not even know what we do not know. Even the best risk management will not help in this situation. In relative uncertainty, we know that a risk exists and we have some partial information helping us to assess and mitigate it. This is where risk management is the most useful. Complete certainty should be included in the project plan and not be a part of risk analysis.

Box 2.6 lists the popular risk types [Walden et al., 2015].

BOX 2.6 POPULAR RISK TYPES [WALDEN ET AL., 2015]

- Safety risk (to patients, health workers, general public)
- Non-acceptance risk (risk of rejection by stakeholders)
- Insurable risk
- Direct property damage risk
- Indirect consequential loss
- Legal liability
- Personnel risk (other than safety) and risk of conflict with unions
- Financial and schedule risks (the hospital wing may not be finished on time …)
- Technical risks (the device may not interface with our server)
- Other …

The best judges of what constitutes risk in each project are the project stakeholders or other invited experts. Managerial experience matters! We need to fend off two extremes: Inexperienced and naïve employees expecting "textbook performance" while an experienced manager will recognize a risk; and the reverse, when an anxious employee wants to classify some unknown as a risk, while an experienced manager will find an easy way to convert the unknown into certainty using work practices. However, in case of doubt, overabundance of caution suggests erring on the side of including the unknown as a risk. Including an unknown as a risk when it is not carries only a small penalty of wasted effort; not recognizing a real risk could be the source of major problems.

Risk is described by two variables: Likelihood and Impact. Likelihood is the probability of the risk occurring. Impact is a measure of risk severity, or the damage (schedule, cost, safety, etc.) if the given risk occurs. After [Lockheed Martin, 2020] both likelihood and impact are estimated on the scales of 1–5, using the following verbal descriptors:

Value	Descriptor of Likelihood or Impact
1	negligible
2	small
3	moderate
4	high
5	very high

Theoretically, we could estimate likelihood and impact based on quantitative evidence. Indeed, if these values are available, they should be used. However, in a typical project we do not have the luxury of sufficient evidence. Experience indicates that the scale 1–5 serves project needs quite well, even if the specific risk values are only estimated as "educated guesses." This author's experience indicates that different stakeholders who are competent in the SoI, may differ in the likelihood or impact estimate by one unit on the scale, but rarely more than that. This level of fidelity is quite sufficient in projects. The awareness of each risk, understanding its mechanism, and the ability to mitigate it before it can cause damage is vastly more important than the ability to assess the risk likelihood or impact exactly.

Each identified risk should be mitigated (prevented, if possible, or reduced) by a well-defined action, and each risk must be allocated to an individual (rather than an organization) as an ongoing responsibility until the risk is resolved. The individual should be responsible for tracking the risk, applying effective mitigations in a timely manner, alarming the project stakeholders at the first sign of the risk appearance, and reporting when it no longer exists.

Opportunity management is the "mirror image" of risk management. Opportunity is the potential enhancement or positive impact that could improve the project ability to deliver the SoI or to meet its performance, cost, schedule, or other objectives [Walden et al., 2015]. While risks represent undesirable events, opportunities represent desirable events that we can utilize to enrich the project or SoI. For example, when designing a new population health activity to address diabetes in patients, a risk may be that a delay in the system design may risk losing patients to both illness and competition, while an early delivery may offer an opportunity to save some patients and take some patients from the competition. The opportunities are characterized by the same likelihood and impact scales with the same numerical values 1–5, with 5 denoting the worst risk and the highest opportunity.

Risk or opportunity management are presented as a table and matrix shown in a template form in Figure 2.10. For each risk in the table, we provide a summary description, likelihood and impact values, a summary of the mitigation strategy, and expected likelihood and impact after mitigation. To repeat, both sets of likelihood and impact values are educated guesses, usually quite sufficient for risk analysis. An identical table and matrix are used for opportunity management, only the word "risk" is replaced by "opportunity," and "mitigation" by "enabling action."

For risk, the sum of likelihood and impact values is called the risk assessment value. Values of 8–10 are regarded as high risk, 6–7 as moderate risk, and 1–5 as low risk. For opportunity, values of 8–10 are regarded as high opportunity, 6–7 as moderate opportunity, and 1–5 as low opportunity. In the matrix in Figure 2.10, they are traditionally shown in red, yellow, and green colors, respectively. Each risk or opportunity position in the matrix is indicated by the risk or opportunity number. Each risk or opportunity should be shown in two cells, one before and the other after planned mitigation or enabling action. An arrow connecting the "before" cell to the "after" cell provides an easy visual means to show each risk (opportunity) mitigation or enablement.

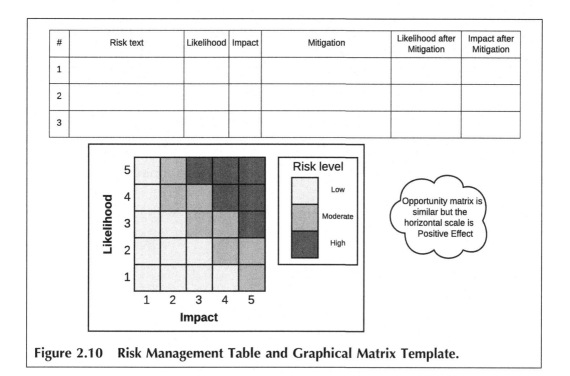

#	Risk text	Likelihood	Impact	Mitigation	Likelihood after Mitigation	Impact after Mitigation
1						
2						
3						

Figure 2.10   Risk Management Table and Graphical Matrix Template.

Figure 2.11 illustrates how the risk analysis works for our example of improving patient discharge from a hospital. For simplicity, only one risk is shown. The project calls for inviting a top SNF manager from each co-operating SNF once a year to proactively negotiate the terms of admissions during the subsequent year, so that the admission of a new patient to a given

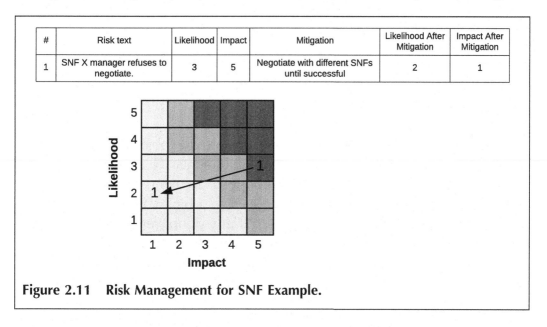

#	Risk text	Likelihood	Impact	Mitigation	Likelihood After Mitigation	Impact After Mitigation
1	SNF X manager refuses to negotiate.	3	5	Negotiate with different SNFs until successful	2	1

Figure 2.11   Risk Management for SNF Example.

SNF could be immediate when a bed is available, free of frustrations and unquestioned by the SNF staff. The identified risk is that one or more SNF managers may refuse to cooperate. The mitigation is to abandon the un-cooperating SNF and select another.

An opportunity in this example may be that if all or most SNFs refuse to cooperate, our hospital may decide to create its own SNF.

For more complex risks/opportunities, the project team should keep a running online document listing for each risk or opportunity:

- The risk or opportunity sequential number, with letter R or O, respectively
- Risk or opportunity description
- Mitigation or enabling strategy
- The likelihood and impact before and after the mitigation or enabling action
- The individual responsible for monitoring and mitigating the risk or opportunity and reporting it to the project manager
- A diary of risk or opportunity monitoring events

2.3.9 *Verification and Validation (V&V)*

As Figure 1.4 illustrates, at this phase of the project, our SoI has been created, architected, and analyzed for risks and opportunities. Now comes the time to check if it is good enough. We do this in two activities: verification and validation, colloquially called V&V. An informal explanation of the difference between the two is[10]:

- Verification ensures the system was built right.
- Validation ensures the right system was built.

The purpose of the **Verification** process is to provide objective evidence that a system or system element satisfies its requirements. To repeat after Section 2.3.2, verification methods include measurement, observation, demonstration, or analysis. Verification must have a binary outcome: Pass or Fail. No other possibility can be allowed. If any doubt remains, it is a clear sign that the requirement statement was not formulated correctly, lacking clarity, precision, single meaning or was too ambiguous, or the verification method was not adequate. If any requirement fails verification, the SoI must be redesigned.

Once all requirements pass their verifications, we advance the project to Validation. **Validation** confirms that project Goals have been achieved, that is that the SoI delivers the expected functionality and performance. Validation is a process of attaining and documenting sufficient evidence to give reasonable[11] assurance that the SoI does (or will do) what was intended and needed [INCOSE, 2019].

Ideally, the validation should be performed by actual intended users during the pilot phase of the new SoI. However, the project stakeholders may be different from implementation stakeholders. Project stakeholders may create new methods, recommendations, procedures, standards, checklists, and others and hand them over to a hospital or clinic or population health team for implementation. This is often the case when interns or students who perform the project during a semester do not have enough time to implement and validate it. In such cases, preliminary validation should be performed using professional judgment of the expert implementation stakeholders. A detailed plan of the SoI buyoff may be needed as a project deliverable.

Good practices of V&V are described by several authors in a joint edition of [INCOSE, 2019].

2.4 Implementation

2.4.1 *Implementation of Future State Design*

Implementation is the final phase of the LHSE process. Here we put to life the new Future State Design. This may involve the following activities (in view of the huge variety of healthcare projects, we do not attempt to provide a complete list, but the following should serve as a good sample):

- Preparation of implementation plan "what needs to be done" (what, when, by whom, how, where). We can define similar Interrogatives for the Implementation phase as those shown in Section 2.3.3 for the project phase.
- Preparation of training materials (slides, videos, manuals, checklists, procedures, standards, etc.)
- Purchase of relevant equipment, materials, or supplies.
- Selection of the trainers and users to be trained, and actual training of the users.
- Ensuring that the training objectives have been achieved (tests at the end of the training if the process is critical).

- Monitoring and mentoring users during the pilot phase or initial activities.
- Coding of the relevant portion of the system IT/EHR.
- Implementation of a helpline if the project involves difficult IT or equipment or steps.
- Measurements of the outcomes for validation purpose.

Besides validation, we recommend a closure of each LHSE project with an explicit summary comparison of relevant system characteristics between the Current State and the Implemented Future State. Examples of characteristics to compare include:

- Safety aspects of patients, health workers, and public
- Medical efficacy of the new system
- Cost, effort, throughput times, waiting
- System capacity
- Degree of burnout
- Satisfaction of stakeholders (best judged by a well-designed survey)

A table comparing these characteristics between the Current State and Implemented Future State should be shown. We use either numerical values, if available, or qualitative descriptors otherwise. Surveys of relevant stakeholders can be used to obtain the response statistics.

2.4.2 Change Management

Every LHSE project introduces some changes into the Current State. Inevitably, there will be individuals who feel comfortable operating in the Current State, and they will be less than enthusiastic about making changes to it. Changes may be scary; the "new and unknown" may be frightening for some individuals. Folks doubt if they will be "up to it" and how they will be able to learn new ways on top of performing their regular work. They may question the need for new solutions and their efficacy. Therefore, a part of the LHSE process is to be able to persuade all stakeholders that investment of time and energy in the new system will be beneficial to patients, stakeholders, and the institution. Medical and healthcare professionals tend to be well educated and accepting of evidence. A strong evidence for improving patient safety, worker safety, or quality of care is usually sufficiently persuasive. If the project has strong financial aspects, evidence can be provided by a business case, comparing the cost of doing nothing (and paying for consequences of inaction) with the cost of implementing the proposed solution. Simple Payback Period and Return on Investment are two popular metrics used in business cases.

The body of knowledge on how to accomplish the change from the Current State to a Future State is called Change Management. It is beyond the scope of the present text and can be found easily in numerous textbooks and Internet postings. It is a standard component of Lean transformations. Good examples can be found in [Graban, 2012] for hospitals and in [Womack and Jones, 1996] for non-healthcare companies. [Gladwell, 2000] provides a fascinating discussion of persuasion techniques.

We emphasize one critical point, a word of caution. Namely, LHSE professionals tend to be regarded as a "foreign body" among medical professionals. We are trained to discover a system's issues and problems, wastes, and bottlenecks, and usually are eager to offer better solutions. But the key to success are the words "offer" and "evidence" rather than "push." We should never attempt to force our solutions onto the local healthcare and medical stakeholders, as this will only alienate folks. This comment applies particularly to young graduates of academic HSE programs who are full of enthusiasm and knowledge they just gained in school and eager to make changes, but still lack the wisdom of effective persuasion that comes only from experience.

2.4.3 Sharing Success with Sister Organizations

As stated earlier, healthcare projects are often performed by a small team at a single clinic, hospital department, laboratory department or a local pharmacy. After validating project results in that location, it makes sense to share it with all sister organizations in the same medical system[12]. Sharing is the least expensive method of dissemination. It can rapidly bring the new capabilities or performance to all units in the institution, thus, increasing the competitiveness of the entire institution. The sharing replaces unhealthy rivalry with positive energy of teaming. It also prevents the high costs of "reinventing the wheel." The institution incentives should strongly promote such sharing. Each large medical system should have an infrastructure for the sharing, including:

- A means of announcing successful projects, for example, a dedicated website, or a newsletter.
- Electronic means for online training stakeholders in sister institutions.

■ Shared electronic database for dissemination of the materials.

■ Periodic meetings of like stakeholders from sister institutions to compare their operations, challenges, and achievements.

■ A person in charge of coordinating the above activities.

■ Finally, if a given project is particularly successful, the author should be incentivized to present it as a professional publication to a healthcare journal or a conference.

2.4.4 Ethics

Assuring patient wellness and treating sick patients is surely among the most ethical human activities. The LHSE process would not be complete without mentioning the ethical aspects of the project. In every project we should explain why the project (or the SoI) is based on a solid ethical framework, and whom and how it will benefit. Since we do not have a distinct "healthcare" or "LHSE" code of ethics, we should relate the SoI to the next closest thing, namely the Code of Medical Ethics [AMA] shown in Box 2.7. The Box lists the ethical code under 12 headings, each being a link to the corresponding clarifying AMA text (and can be googled as such).

BOX 2.7   CODE OF MEDICAL ETHICS.

■ Principles of Medical Ethics (autonomy of patient in decision making, nonmaleficence, beneficence, and justice)
■ Ethics of Patient–Physician Relationships
■ Ethics of Consent, Communication & Decision Making
■ Ethics of Privacy, Confidentiality & Medical Records
■ Ethics of Genetics & Reproductive Medicine
■ Ethics of Caring for Patients at the End of Life
■ Ethics of Organ Procurement & Transplantation
■ Ethics of Medical Research & Innovation
■ Ethics for Physicians & the Health of the Community
■ Ethics of Professional Self-Regulation
■ Ethics of Interprofessional Relationships
■ Ethics of Financing & Delivery of Health Care

Notes

1 This author is a professor of systems engineering, now specializing in healthcare systems engineering, with over four decades of academic experience. During the first three decades, he insisted that master's capstone projects be presented by students both in a professional written report and as a Power Point presentation. Having observed the steadily declining writing skills of students over the years and the frustratingly long time it took to edit the reports to bring them to a professional standard, the author realized that the time could be better spent on addressing the subject matter. Thus, in 2014, he made a radical decision to make written reports optional, and require only comprehensive 50–60 slide Power Point presentations of projects. The reader of the present book is invited to see sample presentations by graduate students on the page https://cse.lmu.edu/graduateprograms/hse/msstudentcapstoneprojects/. For this reason, the author recommends that LHSE healthcare projects carried out in healthcare institutions be documented and presented using Power Point slides. Of course, appendices to the presentations should contain detailed evidence.

2 including undocumented individuals, as the COVID-19 pandemic dramatically demonstrated.

3 For example, in the recent COVID-19 pandemic, instead of thinking about the basics (protection from infection, testing for infection, and treatment of virus-infected patients), Systems Thinking would push us to think of the entire pandemic, including all medical staff involved in diagnosis and treatment of infected patients; infection characteristics; protections from infection; health risks to providers and the public; testing quality; test facilities and capacity issues; herd immunity; mortality rates; body disposals; hospital admissions and capacity issues; ambulance capacity; social distancing; protective equipment; effect on global, national, and local economy and economy opening criteria; travel and gatherings; help to unemployed and struggling companies, and others. Each reader who went through the pandemic hardships knows the list and could add words to it.

4 The author was involved in a year-long study of a major clinical laboratory and confirms from first-hand experience that each of the fragmentation events (a-h) actually took place.

5 These are only goals. Requirements would be formulated from the goals as the next project phase, written with a higher degree of formalism, to make them verifiable in a binary way: passed or failed. Normally, each requirement would precisely state the degree of needed implementation, the deadline, etc. Requirements are covered in detail in Section 2.3.2.

6 The ability to integrate fragmented elements across interfaces in a multi-disciplinary system was the original stimulating idea for inventing systems engineering.

7 and the last slide in this section of the project presentation slide deck.

8 It is a bad practice to allow some "smart aleck," typically the most senior manager present, to impose his/her solution idea, no matter how good, onto the project team at the beginning of the project without first considering all reasonable alternatives.

9 This author recommends using whatever combination of standard views makes the concept clear, and not paying too much attention to enforced adherence to the purity of DODAF views.

10 A quote often attributed to Peter Drucker: "Managers do things right. Leaders do right things."

11 The word "reasonable" has legal meaning and is used in legal cases, denoting that "a reasonably experienced, educated and competent individual would confirm that...."
12 This author strongly believes in broad and free sharing of healthcare and medical knowledge, as it benefits humanity. Therefore, he recommends placing as few limitations on dissemination of such materials as possible.

Chapter 3

Lean Enablers for Healthcare Delivery Projects

Contents

This chapter includes 63 Lean Enablers for Healthcare Projects. Each Enabler represents a separate project improving a workflow, or care, or an aspect of operations. Each Enabler includes a summary of the main steps of the LHSE process used. Each is called a Lean Enabler because it is based on Lean thinking: promoting value while reducing waste, following the well-established methodology [Oppenheim, 2011; Oehmen, 2012]. The Lean Enablers are listed for all clinical environments, in the order presented in the Contents above.

Each Lean Enabler is organized into a table with the following rows:

■ **Project Title**

■ **Challenge(s)/Waste(s)**

The box identifies typical challenges and wastes. A challenge is the problem, factor, or environment that prevents success, causes frustrations and burnout, and contributes to wastes. The wastes listed follow the standard Lean categorization of waste [Womack, 1996].

■ **Goal(s)/Solution(s) proposed**

This box lists the project improvement goals and key aspects of the suggested solution.

■ **System of Interest (SoI) and stakeholders**

The SoI is the system of people, organizations (such as labs), and tools (including EHR) of interest. Stakeholders are the major individuals, departments or organizations, and elements that contribute to the SoI fragmentation and should be included in the N^2 matrix.

■ **In scope**

The in-scope denotes the project elements, activities, or stakeholders that are subject to the project steps.

■ **Externalities**

This box lists the elements that may affect or be affected by our SoI, but are not a part of the SoI.

■ **Out of scope**

The out-of-scope denotes the project elements, activities, or stakeholders that are excluded from project steps.

■ **Major risks**

Both major risks during the project execution and those to be expected from project results are listed and should be mitigated in the project.

■ **Value/Expected benefits**

This box lists the project value and major benefits from the project.

■ **Literature review**

The literature cited either supports the project intent or is recommended as a background reading for the project. "Not available" means that the author was unable to identify any relevant citation. All citations listed in Chapter 3 tables are also listed in the References Chapter.

■ **Notes**

This blank box provides space for reader's notes.

Note: While this author's lifetime experience indicates that healthcare problems tend to be similar in different healthcare institutions (for example, almost all clinics struggle with similar scheduling problems), some differences due to local conditions are inevitable. Therefore, the reader should use his/her own critical judgment and interpretations of the items listed in the following tables. The items are listed as examples only and are most definitely open to change based on local conditions. This refers particularly to the boxes in the tables labeled System of Interest, Stakeholders, In-scope, Externalities, and Out-of-scope. Individual projects may use different granularity of these items, and different partitions between them, so the items listed should be interpreted only as examples. We suggest that when the reader struggles with these project definitions in a specific project, these boxes should be temporarily left blank and completed at a later time, after the project knowledge matures. In other words: do not let these items slow down the rest of the project.

3.1 Clinics

Project Title	3.1.1 Improve Scheduling in Clinics
Challenge/Wastes	The waste of waiting by patients, safety risks; no shows and overbooking waste; overburden of providers; unbalanced demand and supply of medical services; delays in the day because of random mix of severe and light cases; delays waiting for translator; unmet demand variation; underutilized telemedicine.
Goals/Proposed solutions:	1. Train schedulers to be knowledgeable in screening and scheduling of patients. 2. Schedule to reduce providers' burnout. Allocate frequent time blocks for closing charts and emailing. 3. Schedule patients as soon as possible based on their acuity and clinic statistics. 4. Use past statistics to learn how to balance no shows and overbooking. 5. Schedule physician assistants and nurses instead of MDs for low-acuity cases. 6. Schedule based on severity: light cases first in the day. 7. Schedule non-English speakers together by language, for easy connection and utilization of online translators. 8. Remind patients twice about the appointment, send card one week and a text message 1–2 days prior to appointment via communication method of their choice. 9. Sign flexible contracts with providers to deal with demand variation. 10. Promote telemedicine to unload clinics.

(Continued)

Sol and stakeholders	Scheduler(s) and clinic staff.
In-scope	All activities in the clinic.
Externalities	Outside testing facilities, hospitals, pharmacies.
Out of scope	Scheduling of tests and activities outside of the clinic.
Major risks	1. Patient with severe medical case scheduled to a provider who is not an MD (a PA or RN). 2. Severe-case patient made to wait for appointment.
Value/Expected benefits	Better effective capacity of the clinic, better utilization of resources without adding new resources, more patient-centric care and better patient wellness, fewer frustrations, and reduced burnout of medical staff
Literature review	1. Ansell, D., Crispo, J.A.G., Simard, B. et al. *Interventions to reduce wait times for primary care appointments: A systematic review.* BMC Health Services Research, Vol 17, pg 295. 2017. 2. Brandenburg, L., Gabow, P., Steele, G., Toussaint, J., Tyson, B. *Innovation and Best Practices in Health Care Scheduling.* Institute of Medicine of the National Academies. 2015.
Notes	

Project Title	3.1.2 Reduce Waste of Empty Exam Rooms and Improve Room Utilization
Challenge/Wastes	Poor utilization of capacity; many exam rooms empty during working hours; underutilized nurses; waiting by all: patients and providers.
Goals/Proposed solutions:	1. If the present architecture is corridor-based, change to island architecture with central island for providers and computers, with full visibility of exam rooms, if feasible. 2. Drop the practice of a part-time doctor having a dedicated nurse. Change to shared nurses among providers for better utilization. 3. Drop the practice of exclusive use of 2–4 exam rooms per doctor. Make all exam rooms usable by all providers, whichever is available at the time. Install same standard equipment and supplies in most rooms (perhaps equip one exam room for minor procedures). 4. Architect the clinic to provide maximum visibility of exam rooms, patient status, and activities. 5. Clean room ASAP after last patient, bring next patient in and do vitals and EHR checks (vaccinations, tests due, etc.) right away. 6. Implement electronic visual controls for better room and provider utilization.
Sol and stakeholders	Providers and rooms in clinic.
In-scope	Architecting of clinic spaces, management of clinic medical and staff resources.
Externalities	Activities outside of clinic.

(Continued)

Out of scope	Seeking budgets to implement this project.
Major risks	Rebellion of the doctors who are used to having dedicated exam rooms and nurses.
Value/Expected benefits	1. Better utilization of clinic resources. 2. Higher revenues. 3. Shorter waits for appointments and less health risk to patients. 4. Higher patient satisfaction. 5. More competitive position.
Literature review	Kaiser Permanente, https://www.hdrinc.com/ portfolio/kaiser-permanente-re-imagining-ambulatory-design, accessed Sept. 11, 2020.
Notes	

Project Title	3.1.3 Leverage Technology to Provide Telemedicine, Consulting, and Translation Services
Challenge/Wastes	1. The waste of many in-person visits when telemedicine visits would be medically sufficient and more convenient for patients. 2. Translation by telephone only, while both patents and providers prefer video in addition to audio.
Goals/Proposed solutions:	1. Install TV monitors connected to Internet in as many exam rooms as possible. 2. Install a collection of medical education videos for patients to watch while waiting, and on doctor's instructions. 3. Play videos promoting vaccinations. 4. Provide internet connection and all popular zoom-like software (Signal, WhatsApp, WebEx) to providers in their offices for telemedicine. 5. Train providers in the use of telemedicine technology. 6. Offer online self-taught training to patients. 7. Use the exam room TV for connections to consultants, translators, and for education of patient in real time. 8. Popularize and even distribute to patients the devices for measuring vitals: blood pressure, glucose, oxygen, and even electronic stethoscope/otoscope for use by patients at home in preparation for an online or phone visit.
Sol and stakeholders	All clinic providers and the administrators who sponsor and manage clinic technology.
In-scope	Internet-connected TVs in exam rooms, and communications software in doctors' offices.

(*Continued*)

Externalities	External consultants, translators, technology vendors.
Out of scope	Contracts with consultants, translators, technology vendors.
Major risks	1. Psychological resistance from providers, particularly older generation. 2. Imperfect technology. 3. Interruptions in Internet service.
Value/Expected benefits	1. Telemedicine provides better utilization of medical resources in clinic. 2. More convenient to most patients. 3. Use of telemedicine from home eliminates the risk of infections. 4. Ability to show educational videos to patients, which translates into better general wellness of the clinic patient population 5. Higher competitiveness of clinic.
Literature review	Serper, M., Volk, M.L., *Current and Future Applications of Telemedicine Optimize the Delivery of Care in Chronic Liver Disease.* American Gastroenterology Association, 2018.
Notes	

Project Title	3.1.4 Architect Clinic Spaces so that Doctors' Offices Are Clustered Together for Easier Coordination
Challenge/Wastes	Traditional architecture of a doctor's office being close to his/her exam rooms but in separation from other offices contributes to isolation of providers from each other and fragmentation of healthcare.
Goals/Proposed solutions:	1. Rearchitect spaces to cluster doctors' offices close by. Microwave and coffee station should be in the work area. 2. Each doctor to have his/her computer and private space in the office. 3. Medical library can be shared. 4. Promote real-time quick informal mutual consults (vastly increasing in criticality given the growth of medical knowledge). 5. Promotes real-time coordination which is helpful in care integration and continuity. 6. The new architecture is conducive to efficient department meetings and common training sessions. 7. Conducive to collegiality and mutual support in burnout situations.
Sol and stakeholders	MDs and physician assistants, administrators in charge of providers.
In-scope	Placement of providers' offices, equipment (computers, bookshelves) in doctors' office.
Externalities	Patient areas, nurse stations, Internet technology.
Out of scope	N.A.
Major risks	Resistance from some traditional providers.
Value/Expected benefits	1. Easy real-time mutual consults (vastly increasing in criticality given the growth of medical knowledge).

(Continued)

	2. Better real-time coordination, conducive to care integration and continuity. 3. Easier organization of department meetings and training sessions. 4. Higher levels of collegiality and mutual support in burnout situations. 5. Improved socializing environment (common microwave and coffee station) 6. Shared cost and, therefore, richer medical library.
Literature review	McGough, P.M., Jaffy, M.B., Norris, T.E., Sheffield, P., Shumway, M. *Redesigning Your Workspace to Support Team-Based Care*. American Academy of Family Physicians, 2013.
Notes	

Project Title	3.1.5 Introduce Nurse Navigator/Coordinator ("N/C") Position to Guide Patients through Fragmented Complex Care Steps (e.g., In the Adolescent and Young Adult Oncology Clinics, Guiding through Oncology, Other Medical Activities, Social Work, Fertility Preservation, Mental Health, and Financial Advising)
Challenge/Wastes	Many patients are unable to follow instructions for pursuing complex care activities, are too intimidated, scared and fail to pursue care, with serious and sometimes morbid consequences.
Goals/Proposed solutions:	1. A N/C should be designated and trained to monitor, advise, and guide each patient throughout the system, make real-time entries, and send notifications to patients. 2. EHR must be modified to provide easy visibility of patient progress and status. 3. The entire care should be integrated using SIPOC tools to define the Sources-Inputs-Process-Outputs-Destinations at each care step. All stakeholders should be trained to assure common understanding of the SIPOCs. 4. The patients should be captured into the system at the beginning of the care and monitored until they either elect to drop out or the care process ends.
Sol and stakeholders	1. N/C staff. 2. Trainers of the N/C staff. 3. Managers or representatives of all departments involved in the care 4. Care experts. 5. IT EHR staff making system modifications.
In-scope	All care activities, EHR.

(*Continued*)

Externalities	Medical and social care departments which are not a part of the designated care flow.
Out of scope	Internal management of different care departments.
Major risks	1. "Dropped balls," patient who do not enroll into or follow the N/C instructions. 2. The number of patients too large for the number of assigned N/C individuals.
Value/Expected benefits	1. Integrated and coordinated care of patients. 2. Less confusion and fear on the part of the patients. 3. Less havoc among providers from different cooperating departments. 4. Less waiting and better medical care of patients. 5. Less overall frustrations, less burnout.
Literature review	1. Speicher, S. https://sean-story.wistia.com/medias/bs62oygize, accessed Sept. 11, 2020. 2. Doucet, S., Luke, A., Splane, J., Azar, R. *Patient Navigation as an Approach to Improve the Integration of Care: The Case of NaviCare/ SoinsNavi.* International Journal of Integrated Care, 2019;19(4):7. 3. Carter, N., Valaitis, R.K., Lam, A., Feather, J., Nicholl, J., Cleghorn, L. *Navigation Delivery Models and Roles Of Navigators in Primary Care: A Scoping Literature Review.* BMC Health Services Research, Vol. 18. pg 96, 2018. 4. Rama, F. D. *Role of a Nurse Navigator and Care Pathways in an Integrated Prostate Cancer Care Program.* Journal of Clinical Pathways, Vol. 5. No. 7. pg 33–38, 2019.
Notes	

Project Title	3.1.6 Keep Evolving EHR for Improved User-Friendliness, Usefulness, Ease of Use, Integrating Patients, Providers, Nurses, Tests, Pharmacies, and Payers across the Globe
Challenge/Wastes	1. Imperfect EHR cause frustrations of users. 2. EHR was designed for billing rather than integration of providers, patients, nurses, tests, pharmacies, payers and researchers, and unless improving, it suffers from rejection of users. 3. Many EHR systems add wasteful data entry and extraction work, do not close the loops, lack interoperability, transportability, and granularity.
Goals/Proposed solutions:	1. Keep evolving and improving the system and apply organizational pressure for continuous system improvements. 2. Stand up a dedicated permanent improvement team. 3. Make the system customizable. 4. Keep increasing user satisfaction and interoperability. 5. Define small projects modifying the system for local users. 6. For patient safety, assure perfect transportability of patient data across systems, states, and countries.
SoI and stakeholders	1. EHR vendor. 2. ITS support group. 3. All users organized into groups (e.g., providers of a given specialty).
In-scope	EHR modifications, user groups.
Externalities	Other EHR systems, other medical centers. Governments.
Out of scope	Purchase of new EHR systems.

(*Continued*)

Major risks	1. Costs. 2. Resistance from EHR vendors. 3. Modifications may destroy commonality and centralization.
Value/Expected benefits	Gradually evolve the system towards the ideal tool for real-time comprehensive access by the largest possible number of users.
Literature review	Klas Arch Collaborative Reports on EMRs, https://klasresearch.com/reports, accessed Sept. 11, 2020.
Notes	

Project Title	3.1.7 Implement Online Real-Time Translation Facilities During Work Hours. Use TVs in Exam Rooms
Challenge/Wastes	1. Lack of translators when needed makes it impossible to communicate with a non-English speaking patient. 2. Lack of translators of rare languages. 3. Telephone translation often imperfect, difficult to understand.
Goals/Proposed solutions:	1. Contract with translators to be on call during the hours specified. Review the languages used by patients who lack English and add translators of these languages to the database. 2. If translator's hours do not cover the clinic working hours, have the scheduler of clinic visits match patients, providers, and translators for common time. 3. Use TV equipment in exam room for translation. 4. Select the translators who use the TV technology used by the clinic (Zoom, WebEx, Facetime, WhatsApp, etc.). 5. Train providers (or office staff) in setting up videoconference for translation purpose.
Sol and stakeholders	Translators, administrators, scheduler, TV, and Internet technology technicians.
In-scope	Quality and availability of translators and equipment.
Externalities	Translator's home offices.
Out of scope	Contracts with translators besides the on-call hours.
Major risks	1. Lack of translators to/from rare languages.

(Continued)

	2. Scheduling of provider, patient, and translator at a common time may delay the patient visit.
Value/Expected benefits	Real-time competent translation is conducive to good medical care and patient satisfaction.
Literature review	1. Masland, M.C., Lou, C., Snowden, L. *Use of Communication Technologies to Cost-Effectively Increase the Availability of Interpretation Services in Healthcare Settings.* Telemedicine Journal and E-Health, 2010. 2. Albrecht, U., Behrends, M., Matthies, H.K., Jan, U.V. *Usage of Multilingual Mobile Translation Applications in Clinical Settings.* JMIR Mhealth Uhealth, 2013.
Notes	

Project Title	3.1.8 Provide On-Site Ancillary Services (Phlebotomy, Small X-Ray, EKG, Ultrasound Device, Pharmacy)
Challenge/Wastes	Lacking on-site ancillary services consume patient time, slow down diagnosis and treatment, and cause motion and transportation waste and inconvenience to patients.
Goals/Proposed solutions:	1. Arrange to have on-site phlebotomy and sample drop off. 2. Have a mobile X-ray. 3. Have a mobile ultrasound and EKG stations. 4. Have a pharmacy, with just-in-time deliveries of medicines not in inventory.
Sol and stakeholders	Patients, providers, phlebotomists, imaging test technicians, pharmacy workers.
In-scope	On-site management of equipment and services.
Externalities	Tests on major equipment and rare tests.
Out of scope	Major equipment (MRI, stationary X-ray, etc.)
Major risks	1. Low patient volume may not assure business case for the equipment and pharmacy. 2. Inventory availability in a small local pharmacy.
Value/Expected benefits	1. Convenience of all services (except major test equipment) being available on site in near real time. 2. Savings of time for patients, providers, Dx, and Tx.
Literature review	Chenoweth, D.H., Garrett, J. *Cost-Effectiveness Analysis of a Worksite Clinic*. American Association of Occupational Health Nurses, Vol. 54. No. 2., February 2006.
Notes	

Project Title	3.1.9 Reduce Repeat Visits to Clinic by Properly Educating the Patient and Printing Comprehensive Instructions for Tx, Medicines, and Behavior
Challenge/Wastes	Avoidable repeat visits cause several wastes: waiting, motion and transportation, system overproduction waste, and defects (safety risk) for patients, as well as capacity overburden and inconvenience to all stakeholders.
Goals/Proposed solutions:	1. Create system for informing the patient on care actions at home, the do's and don'ts, use of medicines, expected cure progress, and others. Design standardized templates, checklists, and forms to print and hand to patient when leaving the clinic. Assure by simple conversation that the patient understands the instructions. 2. Create an IT system for efficient printing of comprehensive visit summary, medicine instructions, follow-up instructions, checklists, warnings, habit change instructions. 3. Have IT implement the forms.
Sol and stakeholders	Providers, clinic staff, IT department.
In-scope	Design of medical instructions, IT project to prepare templates for printing
Externalities	None.
Out of scope	Patient behavior outside of clinic.
Major risks	1. Significant cost and effort for a small independent clinic. 2. Items missing or lacking clarity on the forms may invite malpractice cases.

(Continued)

Value/Expected benefits	1. Reduction of avoidable visits to clinic. 2. Teaching patients about the responsibility for their wellness behaviors and actions.
Literature review	1. Marcus, C. *Strategies for Improving the Quality of Verbal Patient and Family Education: A Review of the Literature and Creation of the EDUCATE model.* Health Psychology and Behavioral Medicine, 2014. 2. Vernon, D., Brown, J.E., Griffiths, E., Nevill, A.M., Pinkney, M., *Reducing Readmission Rates through a Discharge Follow-Up Service.* Future Healthcare Journal, June 2019. (This text is for hospitals, but also applies to clinics).
Notes	

3.2 Hospitals (Except Operating Rooms and Emergency Departments)

Project Title	3.2.1 Streamline Admission to Hospital from ED
Challenge/Wastes	1. Delays in admission of patients to hospital in ED. 2. Overstay of patients in ED, thus, decrease of ED capacity. 3. Safety risks for patients. 4. Overproduction and over-processing. 5. Hospitalist motion waste.
Goals/Proposed solutions:	1. Eliminate the need for hospitalist to come to ED and approve each admission to hospital. Trust ED intensivist and eliminate waiting for hours for hospitalists to come to ED. Hospitalists to review electronic records entered by the ED physician from hospital computer, perhaps only followed by a phone call to the ED MD. 2. Only in rare special cases (e.g., need to look at skin color) a personal visit by hospitalist to ED is justified. 3. Provide visual control or pager signals to hospitalists to initiate the next patient evaluation within, say, 5 minutes from receiving the request to admit the patient to hospital. 4. Admission of ES1 (most severe) and possibly ES2 patients should be automatic; no evaluation needed. 5. Utilize physicians in front-end triage (a physician is required to conduct medical screening examination anyway to immediately assess the severity of the patient. So, might as well do it in the front-end triage). The MD to order tests and preliminary treatment immediately.

(Continued)

	6. Reduce bureaucratic handoffs between ED and hospital staff when admitting the patients. Eliminate silos and territoriality within silos. Allocate shared offices to stakeholders making admission decisions for immediate resolutions. Better: Consolidate decision in one competent trained person.
Sol and stakeholders	ED and hospital administrative and medical staff involved in patient admission to hospital. IT designing visual controls to aid both.
In-scope	Coordination among stakeholders. Integration of fragmented decisions.
Externalities	Transfer of patient to other hospital(s).
Out of scope	Hospital beds at capacity.
Major risks	Misdiagnosis by ED intensivist (expected low likelihood)
Value/Expected benefits	1. Faster admission of patients. 2. Less safety risks. 3. Better utilization of ED and hospital beds.
Literature review	Algauer, A., Rivera, S., Faurote, R. *Patient-Centered Care Transition for Patients Admitted through the ED: Improving Patient and Employee Experience.* Journal of Patient Experience, May 2015.
Notes	

Project Title	**3.2.2 Reduce Waste of Time and Fragmentation by Better Planning, Coordination, and Integration with Cooperating Stakeholders Outside the Hospital**
Challenge/Wastes	1. Waste of time trying to locate the needed stakeholder who is not a full-time employee. 2. Safety risk if needed stakeholder cannot be located. 3. Frustration of hospital staff unable to locate the needed person or organization, and resultant delays.
Goals/Proposed solutions:	1. Improve planning, coordination, and integration with cooperating/associated stakeholders (providers and consults, labs, pharmacy, phlebotomy, transporters, translators, payers, technicians, and others). 2. Construct a user-friendly database of all these stakeholders for immediate access when needed, showing phone and pager numbers, and emails. 3. Improve visibility of activities and people using electronic visual control boards. 4. Organize multidisciplinary medical groups integrated with hospitals and health plans.
Sol and stakeholders	The entire set of cooperating/associated stakeholders (providers and consults, labs, pharmacy, phlebotomy, transporters, translators, payers, technicians, and others).
In-scope	Any stakeholder with whom the hospital has or may cooperate in any way.
Externalities	Individuals and organizations of no cooperation interest to the hospital.

(Continued)

Out of scope	Individuals and organizations of no cooperating interest to the hospital.
Major risks	Excessive time and effort trying to identify contacts of stakeholders.
Value/Expected benefits	1. Ability to contact needed stakeholder in real time. 2. Less waiting waste. 3. Less frustrations. 4. Less safety risk.
Literature review	Enthoven, A.C. *Integrated Delivery Systems: The Cure for Fragmentation*, American Journal of Managed Care, December 2009.
Notes	

Project Title	3.2.3 Rearchitect Large Hospital Spaces into Smaller Units for Better Visibility of Patient Rooms and Providers in Each Unit
Challenge/Wastes	1. Lack of visibility of patients and delayed reaction in case of need. 2. Safety risk. 3. Motion and transportation waste. 4. Waiting waste. 5. Overproduction and over-processing.
Goals/Proposed solutions:	Rearchitect large hospital spaces into smaller units, with nurses and providers' station located centrally in each unit, with all patient rooms well visible, assuring a short walking distance between the station and each room.
SoI and stakeholders	Hospital administration and employees.
In-scope	Entire hospital building and staff. Perhaps deal with one hospital department at a time to minimize disruptions.
Externalities	Buildings outside the hospital.
Out of scope	Activities outside of hospital.
Major risks	Cost of renovation, temporary loss of capacity and revenue.
Value/Expected benefits	1. Vastly better hospital layout, conducive to good visibility of patients. 2. Ability to react to patient needs faster. 3. Less motion and transportation waste. 4. Less safety risk. 5. Less waiting.
Literature review	Reiling, J., Hughes, R.G., Murphy, M.R., *The Impact of Facility Design on Patient Safety.* Patient Safety and Quality: An Evidenced-Based Handbook for Nurses, 2008.
Notes	

Project Title	3.2.4. Shorten the Patient Discharge Time from Hospital Rooms
Challenge/Wastes	Excessive patient discharge time, waiting waste, waste of hospital bed capacity, unhappy patients.
Goals/Proposed solutions:	1. Construct a discharge lounge suitable for both bed-ridden and in-wheelchair patients and execute all discharge activities in the lounge. 2. Improve cooperation among the in-hospital individuals managing discharges, use a nurse navigator. 3. Pre-negotiate patient admission criteria and real-time notifications about available rooms with all cooperating SNFs, hospices, and boarding facilities for quick automatic placement of patients. 4. Pre-negotiate with DME vendors for real-time deliveries of DME to patient destination. 5. Improve proactive communications with family/caretaker to reduce waiting for patient pick up. 6. Issue medication orders early (as soon as the discharge orders are issued) to supply medicines when needed. 7. Create a system of just-in-time EVS services after the patient leaves the hospital room, including early notifications and cleaning and re-supplying.
Sol and stakeholders	Hospital activities and hospital stakeholders involved in patient discharges, plus a manager from each cooperating SNF, boarding facility, hospice, and DME vendor.
In-scope	In-hospital discharge activities, strategic negotiations between the hospital and the above institutions.

(Continued)

Externalities	Insurances and the post-hospital care institutions.
Out of scope	Hospital activities prior to discharge orders, management of the institutions outside the hospital, payers.
Major risks	Managers of cooperating SNFs and other post-hospital care facilities refuse to sign proactive agreements.
Value/Expected benefits	1. Higher availability of hospital beds for new patients, better utilization of hospital rooms, more revenue. 2. Higher satisfaction of patients.
Literature review	1. Bresnick, J. *Patient Navigators Shave Hours from Hospital Discharge Times; Patient Navigators May Be the Key to Reducing Hospital Discharge Times and Preventing Admissions Traffic Jams.* Health IT Analytics, June 30, 2016. 2. Maguire, P. *How to Streamline Discharges. A Medical Center Eliminates Discharge Bottlenecks in the Pharmacy.* Today's Hospitalists, October 2018.
Notes	

Project Title	3.2.5 Reduce Burnout of Providers by Better Integration of Fragmented Care Elements, Better Coordination, Standardization, Checklists, and Training
Challenge/Wastes	Fragmentation of care elements, workflows, time delays in communications, "dropped balls," imperfect communications, and others cause safety risks, imperfect care, delayed care, readmissions, unnecessary repeat visits, and a number of other system imperfections, all of which contribute to provider stress, frustrations, and burnout.
Goals/Proposed solutions:	1. Identify fragmentation issues (fragmented care elements, workflows, time delays in communications, "dropped balls," imperfect communications, and others, and the relevant imperfect interfaces. 2. Use the Lean Healthcare Systems Engineering (LHSE) process to integrate across the interfaces. Formulate and implement mitigations. 3. As the system becomes better integrated, frustrations and risks will be reduced and so will the burnout.
SoI and stakeholders	All individuals and organizations that have been identified as a party to the above fragmentations.
In-scope	Any or all interfaces of two or more fragmented elements.
Externalities	The work elements that are not the subject to the integration effort. Burnout caused by other factors, for example, work overload, excessive overtime, lack of resources, legal exposure, unfriendly management, dysfunctional technology, equipment breakdowns.

(Continued)

Out of scope	Work overload, excessive overtime, lack of resources, legal exposure, unfriendly management, dysfunctional technology, equipment breakdowns.
Major risks	1. Lack of integration solution because of bias in favor of only one side of the interface. 2. "Looking at trees and forgetting about the forest" syndrome.
Value/Expected benefits	Better integration of work elements yields fewer fragmentation issues, better care, fewer frustrations, and less burnout.
Literature review	1. Zubatsky, M., Pettinelli, D., Salas, J., Davis, D. *Associations Between Integrated Care Practice and Burnout Factors of Primary Care Physicians*, Family Medicine, 2018. 2. Smith, C.D., Balatbat, C., Corbridge, S., Dopp, A.L., Fried, J., Harter, R., Landefeld, S., Martin, C.Y., Opelka, F., Sandy, L., Sato, L., Sinsky, C., *Implementing Optimal Team-Based Care to Reduce Clinician Burnout*. National Academy of Medicine, September 2018.
Notes	

Project Title	3.2.6 Reduce Alarm Fatigue
Challenge/Wastes	1. Frequent and aggressive visual and auditory alarms from medical equipment often overwhelm medical staff. 2. This causes alarm fatigue: lower overall cognitive performance and lack of discrimination of critical versus trivial alarms. 3. Patients are exhausted and scared by the alarms, often calling nurses unnecessarily. 4. Safety risks of not reacting to critical alarms in a timely manner.
Goals/Proposed solutions:	1. Create a central alarm monitoring booth in each hospital unit. 2. The booth is to be managed by a technician. 3. The booth is to be enclosed and acoustically isolated. 4. The relevant medical devices issuing alarms are to feed signals by wireless (Bluetooth or Wi-Fi) or inconspicuous hidden wires to the booth monitoring screens. 5. The monitoring system is to allow detailed review of each patient's alarms, as well as overall status for all patients being monitored 6. The technician is to have capability to immediately notify a local nurse, or a backup in emergency. 7. Allocate one technician per shift per booth, plus a roving technician to replace another when needed for breaks, meals, and biological time. 8. Once the alarm monitoring booth is operational, suppress auditory alarms at patient beds and replace them with a well-visible strobe light placed so that it flashes towards the ceiling and not at patients or staff.

(Continued)

	9. Replace individual uncoordinated alarms with intelligent consolidated alarms to reduce the total number of alarms and alarm fatigue.
Sol and stakeholders	1. All patient rooms and beds. 2. All medical equipment emitting alarms. 3. All workers on the hospital floor. 4. IT staff setting up the alarm booth.
In-scope	All visual and auditory alarms from medical equipment.
Externalities	Electronics not related to medical equipment in patient rooms.
Out of scope	Equipment not emitting alarms. Equipment incapable of signaling alarms to remote location.
Major risks	1. Cost of the booth installation. 2. Lack of redundancy or immediacy in technician's calling a nurse about critical alarm.
Value/Expected benefits	1. Quiet environment on hospital floor. 2. Better work environment. 3. Silence in patients' rooms.
Literature review	1. Paine, C.W., Goel, V.V., Ely, E., Stave, C.D., Stemler, S., Zander, M., Bonafide, C.P. *Systematic Review of Physiological Monitor Alarm Characteristics and Pragmatic Interventions to Reduce Alarm Frequency.* Journal of Hospital Medicine, December 2015. 2. Sendelbach, S., Funk, M. *Alarm Fatigue: A Patient Safety Concern.* Advanced Critical Care, 2013. 3. Solet, J.M., Barach, P.R., *Managing Alarm Fatigue in Cardiac Care.* Progress in Pediatric Cardiology, May 2012.
Notes	

Project Title	3.2.7 Improve Efficiency of Rounds with More Efficient Preparation of Patient Records for Rounds
Challenge/Wastes	1. Waste of waiting for patient data needed for rounds to be manually extracted from EHR, typically by a resident. 2. Transcription errors from manual transcription of data. 3. Manual over-processing of the data.
Goals/Proposed solutions:	1. Modify EHR so that a quick printout of relevant patient data needed for rounds is made "with one button." 2. Define the data to be printed out. 3. Print the number of sheets of the data for each patient equal to the number of participants in the rounds (students, residents, doctors, nurses, others). 4. 60 min before the round, print out the data for all patients who will be subject of the upcoming round, to give stakeholders time to review the data.
Sol and stakeholders	EHR team. All participants in rounds.
In-scope	All data needed for the rounds for all patients being reviewed.
Externalities	All other activities in hospital.
Out of scope	EHR system, except for the module extracting the data needed for rounds.
Major risks	IT system failure, printouts not available.

(Continued)

Value/Expected benefits	Availability of patient data for all stakeholders taking parts in the rounds in almost real time. No need to manually extract the data from each EHR record, which is time consuming, prone to transcription errors, and causes delay from extraction time to rounds time.
Literature review	Not available
Notes	

Project Title	3.2.8. Reduce Hospital Readmits
Challenge/Wastes	1. Waste of avoidable repeated hospitalizations. 2. Medical defects requiring readmission.
Goals/Proposed solutions:	1. Do not discharge patients until perfectly stable, and ready to take care of self or by family-caretaker. 2. Assure the patient has proper care available at the destination (home or other facility). 3. Print better (easier to read and more comprehensive) discharge information, with post-hospital care instructions, and follow up actions. Assure the patient/family/caregiver understand the instructions. 4. Instruct the patient/family/caregiver in wound care and hygiene. 5. Explain to each patient/family/caregiver the expected discomforts and healing process and mitigations. 6. Explain the warning signs to watch for when seeing an MD is required. 7. Follow up by phone with patient at home.
Sol and stakeholders	1. Patient/family/caregiver. 2. Attending MD who orders discharge. 3. Discharge nurse and hospital staff. 4. DME vendor, if used.
In-scope	Any medical consideration relevant to patient discharge and readmission.
Externalities	Any consideration not medically relevant to the decision to discharge.

(Continued)

Out of scope	Any medical consideration not relevant to patient discharge.
Major risks	1. Avoidable readmission. 2. Ignored medical condition(s) that lead to readmission.
Value/Expected benefits	1. Elimination of avoidable readmission. 2. Better medical care and less medical risks.
Literature review	1. Vernon, D., Brown, J.E., Griffiths, E., Nevill, A.M., Pinkney, M., *Reducing Readmission Rates through a Discharge Follow-Up Service*. Future Healthcare Journal, June 2019. 2. Leppin, A.L., Gionfriddo, M.R., Kessler, M., Brito, J.P., Mair, F.S., Gallacher, K., Wang, Z., Erwin, P.J., Sylvester, T., Boehmer, K., Ting, H.T., Murad, M.H., Shippee, N.D., Montori, V.M. *Preventing 30-Day Hospital Readmissions: A Systematic Review and Meta-Analysis of Randomized Trials*. The Journal of the American Medical Association Internal Medicine, July 2014.
Notes	

Project Title	3.2.9. Eliminate Conflicting Orders between OR Doctors and Intensivists in Post-OP ICU
Challenge/Wastes	Conflicting and changing orders for care given by OR staff and intensivists in ICU cause medical risks, safety issues, frustrations, and burnout of staff
Goals/Proposed solutions:	1. Change semi-closed ICU to closed ICU for more consistent care. 2. Or continue using semi-closed ICUs but implement close coordination huddles involving both the OR and ICU medical staffs, to agree on the care, including medical orders, checklist, standards. 3. Post-op patients entering the ICU from surgery should be accompanied by relevant medical data (e.g., blood loss).
Sol and stakeholders	Medical personnel in the OR and ICU.
In-scope	Care decisions in post-op ICU.
Externalities	Doctors outside of OR and ICU.
Out of scope	Medical considerations which are outside the OR and ICU care.
Major risks	Inability to achieve consensus between the OR and ICU medical staff.
Value/Expected benefits	1. Better and consistent care for the patient. 2. Less burnout. 3. Shorter stay in the ICU.
Literature review	Chowdhury, D., Duggal, A.K. *Intensive Care Unit Models: Do You Want Them to Be Open or Closed? A Critical Review.* Neurol India, 2017.
Notes	

Project Title	3.2.10. Reduce Hospital Room Turnover Time
Challenge/Wastes	1. Waiting for EVS staff to arrive and start cleaning 2. Waiting by patients for hospital room 3. Safety risks associated with imperfect cleaning of rooms 4. Decreased utilization of hospital capacity
Goals/Proposed solutions:	1. Notify EVS as soon as the patient discharge time from the room is known, to give EVS time to prepare. Follow with a notification when the patient leaves. 2. EVS to prepare everything needed while the patient is still in the room: linen and towels, room supplies, sanitizing supplies, cleaning tools on a convenient cart(s). 3. Practice and perfect Lean changeover techniques (external changeover, internal changeover). 4. Create 5S standards for supplies and materials on cleaning carts. 5. Train EVS in "Lean single minute die exchange," without forcing anyone to work harder or faster. 6. Implement efficient proactive notifications of EVS, best electronically. 7. Develop prioritization standards for EVS crews (regular, STAT, CRITICAL), and cleaning level standards (regular, infectious, pandemic).
Sol and stakeholders	1. EVS staff. 2. Nurses communicating with EVS. 3. Safety officers preparing disinfecting and cleaning standards.
In-scope	1. EVS staff. 2. All supplies, materials used by EVS. 3. Communications with EVS.

(Continued)

	4. Safety policies and standards dealing with EVS. 5. Training of EVS staff.
Externalities	Inventory of cleaning supplies, linen, towels, room consumables.
Out of scope	1. Hospital inventory control. 2. Rooms outside of hospital (e.g. ambulatory spaces if normally not cleaned by EVS)
Major risks	1. Not enough EVS staff for the need. 2. Safety risks caused by rushed and poorly trained EVS staff.
Value/Expected benefits	1. Less time wasted waiting for and cleaning the rooms. 2. Better effective utilization of hospital beds/rooms. 3. Faster medical care delivered to patients waiting for a room.
Literature review	Jafari, M., *Reducing Turnover Time to Improve Efficiency in the Operating Room*. USF Master's Projects and Capstones, 2017 (note: this reference deals with OR turnover, but some tools and concepts also apply to hospital room turnover).
Notes	

Project Title	3.2.11. Reduce Fragmentation in Hospital using a Care Coordinator
Challenge/Wastes	The best care is delivered when it is in perfect coordination among the stakeholders. This is particularly important when the care of a given patient involves numerous activities and people. Fragmentation and poor coordination tend to cause safety risks and massive delays and waiting, rework, overproduction, and waste of motion and transportation.
Goals/Proposed solutions:	1. In complex multi-action treatments, place one provider in position of "Nurse Navigator," or "Care Coordinator" in charge of each patient care. 2. Place one provider in charge of each patient care on a given shift, with perfect coordination between shifts. 3. The person is to coordinate with other providers by "broadest bandwidth" available. 4. The Navigator to always know in real time the patient status, act as patient advocate, anticipating, planning, and coordinating the next action (treatment, test, move, consult, coordination with other stakeholders, etc.), and reduce waiting waste and risks. 5. Modify EHR to enable real-time detailed monitoring of all activities and patient status and provide a screen with all instructions for the next shift.
SoI and stakeholders	All care elements, including humans and tests involved.
In-scope	All care elements involved and all participating people. Also, EHR.

(Continued)

Externalities	Care elements outside of the planned workflows.
Out of scope	Care elements in externalities.
Major risks	1. Imperfect coordination between shifts. 2. Inadequate monitoring in EHR.
Value/Expected benefits	1. Perfect real-time coordination among all stakeholders involved in the given care. Better safety. 2. Eliminated delays and waiting, rework, overproduction, and waste of motion and transportation. 3. Shorter patient stay in the hospital.
Literature review	Berry, L.L., Rock, B.L., Houskamp, B.S., Brueggeman, J., Tucker, L., *Care Coordination for Patients with Complex Health Profiles in Inpatient and Outpatient Settings*, May Foundation for Medical Education and Research, February 2013.
Notes	

Project Title	3.2.12. Increase Overall Quality and Efficiency of Hospital Stay, and Patient Safety using Checklists and Standardization Based on Latest Medical and Healthcare Knowledge
Challenge/Wastes	Lack of standards results in lack of predictability and high variability of care, workload, schedules; and causes massive frustrations, burnout, and all categories of waste.
Goals/Proposed solutions:	Establish a culture that captures each new element of progress in medical and healthcare knowledge into an update in the standards/checklists.
SoI and stakeholders	All stakeholders and organizations that are subject to a given standard or checklist. The culture of standardization should be ubiquitous in hospital environment.
In-scope	All elements subject to the given standard.
Externalities	The elements outside the standard.
Out of scope	Activities not subject to the standard.
Major risks	1. Long approvals and release of a new standard, which destroys the culture of quick updates of standards. 2. "Frozen" obsolete standards, which should be changed or abandoned but remain due to the management inertia.
Value/Expected benefits	Standards represent the currently best-known way to execute work. With constant progress of medical and healthcare knowledge good standards assure stability, consistency, and repeatability.

(Continued)

	Standards should be updated when a better way of doing work is established.
Literature review	Hales, B., Terblanche, M., Fowler, R., Sibbald, W. *Development of Medical Checklists for Improved Quality of Patient Care*. International Journal for Quality in Health Care, Vol. 20. No. 1, February 2008.
Notes	

Project Title	3.2.13. Reduce Fragmentation between Shifts by Introducing Time Overlap during Shift Changes, with Joint Huddle of Both Shifts
Challenge/Wastes	Rushed shift changes offer numerous opportunities for miscommunications, lack of details critical to care, introducing safety risks, and waste of all types.
Goals/Proposed solutions:	1. Demand the arrival of the new shift and departure of the previous shift to be such as to allow for a 10–20 min overlap for an unrushed huddle. 2. The huddle to discuss all relevant patients in the department, particularly urgent, critical, and difficult cases. 3. If in-person participation in a huddle is not possible for whatever season, an extended unrushed phone conversation should be used instead.
Sol and stakeholders	1. Administrators in charge of time allocations for providers. 2. All providers in the hospital who work on a shift basis
In-scope	All providers who work on a shift basis.
Externalities	The providers who work on schedules other than shifts.
Out of scope	The providers who work on schedules other than shifts.
Major risks	1. Demand for overtime pay from unions. 2. Resistance from administration to additional overtime pay. 3. Late arrivals of the new shift people.

(Continued)

Value/Expected benefits	1. Much greater ability to assure care continuum across shift boundaries. 2. Reduction of fragmentation of information about patient care. 3. Greater care safety and effectiveness. 4. Shortened hospital stay and readmission reduction.
Literature review	Yoshida, H., Rutman, L.E., Chen, J., Enriquez, B.K., Woodward, G.A., Mazor, S.S. *Waterfalls and Handoffs: A Novel Physician Staffing Model to Decrease Handoffs in a Pediatric Emergency Department*. Annals of Emergency Medicine – An International Journal, October 2018.
Notes	

Project Title	**3.2.14. Organize Multidisciplinary Medical Groups Integrated with Hospital(s) and Health Plans**
Challenge/Wastes	Ad hoc spontaneous mix of doctors' offices, specialty clinics, and ancillary organizations (testing, specialized diagnosis, and treatments, etc.) require vastly bigger effort of coordination, provider scheduling, hospital privilege management, reimbursements and financial transactions, and other activities. This tends to yield a chaotic, inefficient, and ineffective system, poorer care of patients, more frustrations for all participants and higher burnout. Less transparency in the system. Such a system is confusing to patients.
Goals/Proposed solutions:	1. Promote consolidation of the various stakeholders into as few medical groups and health plans as possible with maximum clarity on all interfaces and interactions. 2. Promote standardization of EHR and other IT and administrative activities and tools for maximum uniformity and effectiveness.
SoI and stakeholders	All stakeholders (individual providers, small clinics, larger clinics, cooperating labs, etc.) associated with a given hospital system.
In-scope	Improvement and streamlining of all relevant interactions and standardization of EHR, scheduling, reimbursements, and other financial and administrative transactions among all members.

(*Continued*)

Externalities	Internal management (not taking part in the above interfaces) of organizations in the consolidated system.
Out of scope	Internal management (not taking part in the above interfaces) of organizations in the consolidated system.
Major risks	1. Resistance from participating members. 2. Slow and frustrating implementation of EHRs. 3. Poor management of the new system, with its new complexities and modalities.
Value/Expected benefits	A medical complex ("group") operating with common standards, streamlined interfaces, with much less waste. Less confusion and greater transparency to patients.
Literature review	Enthoven, A.C., *Integrated Delivery Systems: The Cure for Fragmentation*, American Journal of Managed Care, December 2009.
Notes	

Project Title	3.2.15. Improve Efficiency of New Nurse Hiring. Concretize Activities. Make Approvals Simultaneous by All Stakeholders at a Single Meeting and Eliminate Serial Approvals. Develop Standards and Procedures
Challenge/Wastes	In some medical systems, the process of hiring a new nurse is excessively bureaucratic, with many tedious sequential approvals, iteration loops, and it takes excessive amounts of time and effort. The slow system causes best nurses to seek employment elsewhere.
Goals/Proposed solutions:	1. Vastly streamline the nurse hiring process. 2. Limit the number of people involved in approving a new hire to those truly needed to be involved. 3. Concurrentize all approvals of candidates to a single meeting of all approving managers, held frequently (e.g., weekly or monthly). 4. Standardize the requirements given to the candidates and precisely describe all submissions, documents, verifications, and records that a new candidate must supply. Create a position of a candidate mentor, who will be available to assist the candidates with preparations. 5. Conduct reviews of the documents and interviews of a candidate in a single day. 6. Streamline HR process to be able to hire an approved candidate in 1–2 days. 7. Inform the candidate of the outcome within one day.

(Continued)

	8. Promote this efficient system in industry so that best candidates will apply for the jobs.
Sol and stakeholders	All stakeholders involved in hiring a new nurse. The HR department
In-scope	All steps involved in hiring a nurse.
Externalities	Verification agencies that verify records.
Out of scope	Decisions to hire a new nurse.
Major risks	1. Resistance of bureaucrats 2. Inertia of the HR department.
Value/Expected benefits	Reduction of the nurse hiring process from the present measured in many months to 1–2 weeks, if implemented properly.
Literature review	Healthnovember, *Nurse recruitment: Best practices for hiring top talent*, https://www.wolterskluwer.com/en/expert-insights/nurse-recruitment-best-practices-for-hiring-top-talent, HEALTHNOVEMBER 06, 2018.
Notes	

Project Title	3.2.16. Reduce Waste of Linen and Supplies in Hospital
Challenge/Wastes	Poorly controlled inventory of linen and supplies costs hospitals big losses. Linen and supplies appear lacking, while plenty of them reside "hidden" in lockers, on carts in corridors, on unloaded vendor tracks, etc.
Goals/Proposed solutions:	1. Map the entire workflow of linen from beginning to end. 2. Design the amounts needed for each hospital floor/department and standardize supply and linen locations to reduce motion and transportation waste, as well as excess inventory. 3. Allocate small local inventory and establish visual Kanban levels, resupplying automatically from central storage. 4. Reorder automatically per Kanbans in central storage, resupply from vendors and laundry in real time.
Sol and stakeholders	All linen and supplies used in hospital, plus the lockers and carts used by EVS. Stakeholders: EVS staff, outside linen and supply vendors, inside linen and supply inventory managers, and transporters.
In-scope	Management and in-hospital transportation of linen and supplies.
Externalities	Management of outside vendors, (except their ability to resupply as promised.)
Out of scope	Investigation of stolen linen and supplies.
Major risks	1. Shortages, if inventory supply chain not designed right.

(Continued)

Value/Expected benefits	1. Availability of linen and supplies in small local storage. 2. Efficient resupplies. 3. Efficient use of linen and linen carts. 4. Minimum waste of inventory, motion, and transportation.
Literature review	Jain, K., Sahran, D., Singhal, M., Misra, M.C. *A Novel Way of Linen Management in an Acute Care Surgical Center.* Indian Journal of Surgery, January 2017.
Notes	

3.3 Emergency Departments (ED)

Project Title	3.3.1 Streamline Discharge to Hospital from ED
Challenge/Wastes	Inefficient and bureaucratic process of admitting patients from ED to hospital. The ED intensivist's medical judgment is not trusted, even in the most severe cases of Emergency Severity Index (ESI) of 1, and hospitalist must come down to ED to approve admission of every patient, a task which could be done from a computer in the hospital based on the notes entered by the ED intensivist into EHR record. Then, several administrators (typically called House Supervisor, Bed Utilization Manager, Patient Care Specialist) must approve the admission and select the bed, but if they act sequentially in different locations, the process consumes time, risking patient safety, and lowering the effective capacity of hospital beds.
Goals/Proposed solutions:	1. Trust ED intensivist and eliminate the need for hospitalist to come to ED and approve admission to hospital. Eliminate waiting for hours for hospitalists to come to ED and eliminate patient batching during these visits. Hospitalists to review electronic records entered by the ED physician from hospital location, perhaps also making a phone call to the ED MD to clarify some aspects of care. Admission of ES1 patients should be automatic, if bed is available. 2. Only in rare special cases (e.g. need to look at skin color or a wound) a personal visit is justified.

(Continued)

	3. Provide visual control or pager signals to hospitalists to initiate the next patient evaluation within, say, five minutes from receiving the consult request. 4. Utilize physicians in front-end triage (a physician is required to conduct medical screening examination anyway to immediately assess the severity of the patient.) So, might as well do it in the front-end triage. The MD to order tests and preliminary treatment immediately. 5. Reduce handoffs between ED and Hospital when admitting the patients. Eliminate silos and territoriality within silos. Allocate shared or nearby offices to stakeholders making decisions for immediate simultaneous resolutions: House Supervisor, Bed Utilization Manager, Patient Care Specialist. Better: Consolidate decision making in one competent trained person.
Sol and stakeholders	Hospitalists, ED Intensivists, all administrators involved in admitting a new patient to hospital from ED.
In-scope	Evaluation of patient for admission from ED to hospital. Patient record of Dx and Tx in EHR.
Externalities	Capacity management of ED.
Out of scope	Hospital management other than admissions.
Major risks	1. ED Intensivist too busy to enter comprehensive record into EHR. 2. Resistance from hospital staff to new rules. 3. Hospitalist does not react to ED requests in a timely manner and delays admission.
Value/Expected benefits	1. Saved time of hospitalists batching cases, walking to the ED.

(Continued)

	2. Saved time by sequential decisions of hospital House Supervisor, Bed Utilization Manager, Patient Care Specialist. 3. Better capacity utilization of ED.
Literature review	1. Algauer, A., Rivera, S., Faurote, R. *Patient-Centered Care Transition for Patients Admitted through the ED: Improving Patient and Employee Experience.* Journal of Patient Experience, May 2015. 2. Fuentes, A., Shields, J., Chirumamilla, N., Martinez, M., Kaafarani, H., Yeh, D.D., White, B., Filbin, M., DePesa, C., Velmahos, G., Lee J. *"One-Way-Street" Streamlined Admission of Critically Ill Trauma Patients Reduces Emergency Department Length of Stay.* Internal and Emergency Medicine, October 2017.
Notes	

Project Title	3.3.2. Streamline Patient Discharge to Home, SNF, Hospice, Boarding Facility
	See "Discharge From Hospital, 3.2.4"

Project Title	3.3.3. Implement Visual Controls to Indicate Patient Status (Arrived, Roomed, Seen by Doctor, Waiting for Transfer, In Testing, Admitted to Hospital, Waiting for Discharge, ETC.)
Challenge/Wastes	ED environment is chaotic and highly stressed under the best of circumstances. Lack of self-evident visual information about the patient status, location, and activity greatly contributes to the chaos, and gives rise to safety risks, motion and transportation waste, waiting, defects, and over-processing.
Goals/Proposed solutions:	1. Implement electronic visual control board (a large TV), listing each patient name, diagnosis, severity, location, status (waiting for...), next step(s), special safety notes, and others as well as the attending provider's name and phone. 2. Locate the visual board so that it is not visible to ED visitors, for HIPPA protection. 3. The information on the board must be updated in near-real time. 4. Stakeholders must be trained in who is to update what and when and how.
Sol and stakeholders	All workers in ED. IT support.
In-scope	All ED activities.
Externalities	Hospital outside of ED.
Out of scope	Hospital outside of ED.
Major risks	1. Small risk of confusion during the system deployment.

(*Continued*)

	2. Not updating the board information in real time.
Value/Expected benefits	After the visual board is implemented, the activities become much more orderly. The above wastes are reduced. Stress and burnout are reduced.
Literature review	Verbano, C., Crema, M., Nicosia, F. *Visual Management System to Improve Care Planning and Controlling: The Case of Intensive Care Unit.* Production Planning and Control – The Management of Operations, June 2017.
Notes	

Project Title	3.3.4. Reduce Distractions of Providers in ED
Challenge/Wastes	The ED environment is naturally chaotic, with very sick patients, with family milling around and interrupting providers all the time, with code blue and similar cases needing immediate attention, and others. This is conducive to constant interruptions of providers' work entering or reading data into/from EHR, providing urgent treatments, communicating with other providers, dispensing medicines, and others. If uncontrolled, such interruptions introduce safety risks to patients (and providers, if the patient is infectious), and contribute to stress and burnout.
Goals/Proposed solutions:	1. A provider working at a computer or a nurse dispensing medicines, or provider busy with life-critical activity is to wear a colored hat, or armband, or other self-evident dress element meaning "do not disturb." 2. Give providers engaged in life-critical activities an enclosed space protected from distractions and interruptions. 3. Train stakeholders about non-disruption and non-interruption rules (except for life-saving emergencies, such as code Blue or Red and others.
Sol and stakeholders	Sol: ED.
	All stakeholders working in ED.
In-scope	All activities in ED.
Externalities	Activities outside the ED.
Out of scope	Major mass accidents, which require "all hands-on deck."

(Continued)

Major risks	Too many providers busy with the "do not disturb" signs at a given time, and not enough providers to take care of critical health events. The use of "do not disturb" signs must be reasonable and judicious.
Value/Expected benefits	1. Better environment for providers to do their work calmly, without undue stress. 2. Better patient and provider safety.
Literature review	1. Laxmisan, A., Hakimazada, F., Sayan, O.R., Green, R.A., Zhang, J., Patel, V.L. *The Multitasking Clinician: Decision-Making and Cognitive Demand During and After Team Handoffs in Emergency Care.* International Journal of Medical Informatics, 2007. 2. Rivera, A.J., Karsh, B.T. *Interruptions and Distractions in Healthcare: Review and Reappraisal.* Qual Saf Health Care, August 2010.
Notes	

3.4 Operating Rooms or Suites (OR)

Project Title	3.4.1 Standardize Instruments, Supplies, and Carts for Each Procedure
Challenge/Wastes	1. The traditional culture of OR is to let each surgeon indicate the instruments to prepare for procedure. An increasing number of procedure types use common standard kits (e.g. knee replacements); the kits should be predefined and practiced for all procedure types. 2. To save on purchase of instruments, ORs tend to prepare surgical carts for only the first 2–4 procedures, and then wash the used instruments in a rush for afternoon use. The traditional system is imperfect: 100,000 death from infections in hospitals (not all attributed to OR). This system is increasingly outlawed by regulatory bodies. 3. Circulating nurse is not scrubbed, runs around to fetch needed, missing or forgotten instruments and supplies. Ok if the person fetches the truly needed items, not OK if the items are missing because the surgeon forgot to prescribe them. 4. Many of the above practices are wasteful causing wastes of over-processing, overproduction, defects, motion and transportation, waiting, and inventory.
Goals/Proposed solutions:	1. Standardize the surgical kits/trays for each surgery type. A given kit may have more items than a particular surgeon will use in a specific surgery, which may appear to be wasteful. The savings come from the economy of scale when kits are outsourced, and a reduced need for circulating nurse. If it makes sense, prepare several kits: those used, say, 90% of time, and

(Continued)

	the others, but keep the others packed in sterilized wrapping and sterilized location until needed, so that if not needed, they can be allocated to another procedure. 2. Use a committee of experienced surgeons to define the kit contents. Asking for more than what may be needed by a particular surgeon is OK. 3. Outsource the standard kit preparations. The kits can be sanitized, packaged, and delivered directly to the OR suite by outside vendor(s) who provides the economy of scale. 4. When the new system is in place, perform brief training of surgical stakeholders informing them how the standard kits are organized and how to order them. 5. The system must be flexible and permit a rare exception of a rare instrument, but it must be rare! 6. Some general sets of instruments must be kept on hand for emergency procedures.
SoI and stakeholders	SoI: The specific OR suite. Stakeholders: all surgeons in the OR, all circulating nurses, all OR nurses, all instrument handlers in the hospital.
In-scope	All procedures, except rare emergency ones. All OR surgeons and nurses.
Externalities	The instrument kit vendors.
Out of scope	Internal management of the surgical kit vendors.
Major risks	Resistance to culture change among surgeons of switching to standard kits.

(Continued)

Value/Expected benefits	1. Cheaper OR operations. 2. Fewer errors in instrument sets. 3. Less need (if at all) for circulating nurse. 4. Benefits in surgery and scheduling from standardization and consistency. 5. Better safety from infections. 6. Less overall waste.
Literature review	1. Charnow, C., Modi, P., Sage, A., Staton, M. *Analysis of the Instrument Picking Process in a Case Cart System at the University of Michigan Hospital.* University of Michigan Health System: Program and Operations Analysis, 2010. 2. Balch, H., *The Front Line: Think Outside the Tray and Make the Most of Your Sterile Processing Career*, Ultra Clean Sytems, Incorporated, 2020.
Notes	

Project Title	3.4.2. Use More ORs in the OR Suite for Easier Scheduling and Safer Operations
Challenge/Wastes	Hospitals often wish to limit surgeries to only a few OR rooms in an attempt to minimize the cost of staffing. Packing surgeries into a few rooms (while other rooms are idle) throughout the day inevitably causes tight scheduling, resulting in never-ending room-staff-patient-equipment-overtime scheduling battles. With tight scheduling, any delay in a case propagates through all subsequent cases in the scheduled room, causing stress, burnout, and safety risks.
Goals/Proposed solutions:	The staff can be managed at the same levels using more physical ORs with proper scheduling and moving the staff between appropriate rooms. Better to equip as many ORs as possible with general surgery equipment (with some exceptions, such as robots), then utilize more or all these rooms with time buffers between cases, without replicating staff. This would make scheduling vastly easier, eliminating the rush, lowering the stress of all stakeholders, allowing for inevitable time variability and complexity of cases, lowering stress; thus, increasing both patient and surgeon safety. A well thought out block schedule can also help to ensure that all of the rooms are utilized in an efficient manner.
SoI and stakeholders	SoI: All ORs in the Suite. Stakeholders: Scheduler, OR medical staff.
In-scope	Scheduling of OR medical staff, rooms, patients, equipment, overtime.
Externalities	Activities outside of OR.
Out of scope	Patients.

(Continued)

Major risks	This initiative will provide opportunity to increase safety and reduce scheduling risks.
Value/Expected benefits	Easier scheduling of surgeries. Less stress among OR staff. Less burnout. Less domino effect of delays. Better safety.
Literature review	Byczkowski, M., *Collaborating for a Better Tomorrow: The Operating Room of the Future,* www.digitalistmag.com, accessed Sept. 11, 2020.
Notes	

Project Title	3.4.3. (Applicable If Project 3.4.1 Not Implemented) Buy More Instruments to Last the Day, Save on Sterilization Staff during the Surgery Shifts, and Sterilize (Possibly Outsource) during the Night
Challenge/Wastes	1. To save on purchase of instruments, some ORs tend to prepare surgical trays for only the first 2–4 procedures, and then wash the used instruments in a rush for afternoon use. The system is imperfect: 100,000 death from infections in hospitals (not all but some attributed to OR) 2. Errors in rushed instrument delivery are inevitable, so the circulating nurse runs around to fetch missing instruments and supplies. 3. The above practices are wasteful in all respects: safety risks, wastes of over-processing, overproduction, defects, motion and transportation, waiting, and inventory.
Goals/Proposed solutions:	1. Make a one-time purchase of enough instruments and trays and kits to last the entire day in all ORs used. 2. Between the surgeries, take the used instruments on a cart outside, but perform sterilization and prepping carts for next day on a night shift, carefully, without rush (or better, outsource the task to an external vendor). 3. Use only the minimum required staff on the night shift
SoI and stakeholders	SoI: OR system. Stakeholders: OR management, purchasing department. Surgical cart transportation and instrument sterilization workers. Circulating nurses.
In-scope	Management of surgical instruments.

(Continued)

Externalities	Sterilization vendors.
Out of scope	Management of vendors' companies.
Major risks	During the implementation of the new system: Risk of running out of instruments and delays in surgical cart preparations.
Value/Expected benefits	1. Enough instruments and carts to last the day. 2. No need to cycle instruments in a rush. 3. Lowered patient safety risks and infections. 4. Fewer expenses on sterilization and transportation staff. 5. Less stress and burnout.
Literature review	Balch, H., *The Front Line: Think Outside the Tray and Make the Most of Your Sterile Processing Career*, Ultra Clean Sytems, Incorporated, 2020.
Notes	

Project Title	**3.4.4 Make Real Effort to Remind Out-Patients to Be on Time, on Empty Stomach, Following the Prescribed Medicine Regiment – to Avoid Procedure Cancellation**
Challenge/Wastes	Any patient scheduled for surgery who violates the surgery preparation regiment (eating, drinking, medicines) or who is late to the pre-op admissions causes a domino effect of rescheduling and wastes expensive OR human and material resources.
Goals/Proposed solutions:	1. During pre-op visit explain to the patient/family all surgery preparation rules in the easy-to-understand language. Make sure the patient/family understands. Use translators if needed. 2. Send reminders by email/voice phone 3, 2, 1 days before surgery. Remind about not eating and other rules.
Sol and stakeholders	Patient and all OR stakeholders.
In-scope	Reminders 3, 2, 1 days before surgery.
Externalities	Medical conditions not affecting or not affected by the surgery.
Out of scope	Home life of the patient.
Major risks	The patient/family may ignore the reminders and fail to show up or to be properly prepared.
Value/Expected benefits	1. Better utilization of expensive OR human and equipment resources. 2. Better safety for the patient to have surgery without delays.

(Continued)

Literature review	1. Hovlid, E., Plessen, C.V., Haug, K., Aslaksen, A.B., Bukve, O. *A New Pathway for Elective Surgery to Reduce Cancellation Rates.* BMC Health Services Research, 2012. 2. Caesar, U., Karlsson, J., Olsson, L., Samuelsson, K., Hannsson-Olofsson, E. *Incidence and Root Causes of Cancellations for Elective Orthopaedic Procedures: A Single Center Experience of 17,625 Consecutive Cases.* Patient Safety in Surgery, 2014.
Notes	

Project Title	3.4.5. Influence Medicine Manufacturers to Standardize Containers for Safety
Challenge/Wastes	Medicines used in anesthesia are packaged in similarly looking containers, with similarly looking color caps (e.g. light blue and dark blue). In a rush of surgery mistakes are possible, causing mortal risks to patients.
Goals/Proposed solutions:	Working through FDA and larger medical associations for better leverage and power, convince drug manufacturers to use distinctly looking and standardized containers for all drugs used in anesthesia. (This topic is controversial: see arguments for and against color-coding medication labels; see Literature review in this table)
Sol and stakeholders	1. Pharma companies making drugs used in anesthesia. 2. Medical associations that interact with the pharma. 3. FDA.
In-scope	All look-alike drug containers used in anesthesia.
Externalities	FDA.
Out of scope	Other medicines.
Major risks	Failure to convince the stakeholders to act.
Value/Expected benefits	Elimination of the risk of using a wrong drug.
Literature review	1. Janik, L.S., Vender, J.S. *2020 Pro/Con Debate: Color-Coded Medication Labels – PRO: Color-Coded Medication Labels Improve Patient Safety.* APSF, 2020. 2. Grissinger, M., Litman, R.S. *Pro/Con Debate: Color-Coded Medication Labels – CON: Anesthesia Drugs Should NOT Be Color-Coded.* APSF, 2020.
Notes	

3.5 Pharmacies

Project Title	3.5.1 Rearchitect Pharmacy Floor Plan for Lean Flow
Challenge/Wastes	Pharmacy physical layout has a huge effect on efficiency. Poorly architected layout causes bottlenecks, lost orders, excessive walking by staff, waiting by patients and waiting of staff for each other, and lots of stress, frustrations, and burnout. Well-laid out layout is conducive to a "moving line" lean flow, synchronized per common takt time.
Goals/Proposed solutions:	1. Design a floor plan so that the flow of medicines from order to handoff to patient or destination storage is like a "moving line" Lean flow, synchronized per common takt time. The workpieces do not need to be on an actual moving line and can be pushed/pulled by hand, but the timing and synchronization should emulate a moving line. 2. Balance the line to assure constant takt time. Place as many concurrent workstations in slow processes as needed to match the common takt time. 3. Linear or L-shaped or U-shaped flows are OK, if they are cleanly organized. 4. Move the orders which require doctor's special approval or corrections offline in order not to delay the flow, and designate a dedicated person to interact with the providers. 5. Place medication inventory in a centralized location to minimize walking. 6. Place the most common medications at nearest locations, with less common farther away. 7. Study and optimize staff motion.

(Continued)

SoI and stakeholders	SoI: Pharmacy. Stakeholders: pharmacy employees.
In-scope	Organization of work in pharmacy.
Externalities	Medicine deliveries.
Out of scope	Deliveries of medicines from wholesaler.
Major risks	During the transition from old to new layout, the work may be confusing and chaotic, so the transition should be accomplished during off hours.
Value/Expected benefits	Significant improvement in pharmacy flow, efficiency, predictability, capacity, and work satisfaction.
Literature review	1. Lin, A.C., Jang, R., Sedani, D., Thomas, S., Barker, K.N., Flynn, E.A. *Re-Engineering a Pharmacy Work System and Layout to Facilitate Patient Counseling.* American Journal of Health-System Pharmacy, 1996. 2. Al-Araidah, O., Momani, A., Khasawneh, M., Momani, M. *Lead-Time Reduction Utilizing Lean Tools Applied to Healthcare: The Inpatient Pharmacy at a Local Hospital.* Journal for Healthcare Quality, 2009. 3. Sullivan, P., Soefje, S., Reinhart, D., McGeary, C., Cabie, E.D. *Using Lean Methodology to Improve Productivity in a Hospital Oncology Pharmacy.* American Journal of Health-System Pharmacy, 2014.
Notes	

Project Title	3.5.2. Cross Train Staff with Downward Skills to Balance the Line (Pharmacist to Help Technicians, All to Help Clerks, as Needed)
Challenge/Wastes	In a busy and chaotic pharmacy, there are times when one person with higher skills (e.g., pharmacist) has no immediate task to do, while a person with lower skills (e.g., technician) is overloaded. This contributes to bottlenecks, waiting waste, and stress.
Goals/Proposed solutions:	Train pharmacists in all skills of technicians (filling the prescriptions, managing medicine inventory, possibly calling providers to verify prescriptions) and clerks (accepting orders, locating and handing medicines to customers and ringing the sales), so that any higher-skill person could perform the work of lower skill. (But the cross-training can be performed only downward: It is illegal to allow a clerk to do the job of a technician or pharmacist, and a technician to do the job of a pharmacist).
Sol and stakeholders	Pharmacy staff
In-scope	Downward cross-training
Externalities	Activities outside of pharmacy.
Out of scope	None.
Major risks	Errors made by poorly trained individuals.
Value/Expected benefits	1. Better utilization of pharmacy personnel and better collegiality. 2. Less waiting waste. 3. Faster throughput. 4. Higher effective capacity. 5. Higher competitiveness of the pharmacy.

(Continued)

Literature review	1. Ninan, N., Roy, J.C., Thomas, M.R. *Benefits of Cross-Training: Scale Development and Validity.* Prabandhan Indian Journal of Management, June 2019. 2. Robinson, E.T., Schafermeyer, K.W. *Cross Training of Hospital Pharmacy Technicians.* Pharmacy Practice Management Quarterly, 1996. 3. Sinclair, A., Eyre, C., Shuard, R., Correa, J., Guerin, *A. Introduction of Pharmacy Technicians onto a Busy Oncology Ward as Part of the Nursing Team.* European Journal of Hospital Pharmacy. 2018.
Notes	

Project Title	3.5.3. Implement Visual Control Boards in Pharmacy
Challenge/Wastes	Without electronic control boards, the work progress of any order is effectively invisible. The work tends to be chaotic, stressful, and inevitably causes waiting waste. In busy pharmacies, some orders may appear "lost."
Goals/Proposed solutions:	1. Implement visual control board for tracking every order from beginning to the end, showing the status. 2. Make the boards visible to all staff in pharmacy. 3. Display idle orders (waiting for resupply of medicine, or for interaction with provider) as such. 4. Interface scanners to the boards for easy automatic updates. 5. On the public board (in the waiting room) display customer name for the medicine orders completed, as well as the expected throughput time.
Sol and stakeholders	Sol: Electronic visual control boards Stakeholders: all pharmacy employees.
In-scope	Information interfaced with and displayed on the internal pharmacy boards and on public board in the waiting room (only the names in public spaces).
Externalities	None.
Out of scope	None.
Major risks	Downtime of the electronics.
Value/Expected benefits	1. Full visibility of each order status. 2. Better flow. 3. Faster throughput and less waiting waste. 4. No waste of "dropped balls." 5. Less frustrations.

(Continued)

Literature review	1. Pharmacy Technology, https://www.pharmacytechnologysolutions.ca/pharmaclik-rx-doc/Content/Workflow/Workflow%20Tab.htm, accessed Sept. 11, 2020 2. Computertalk, *Key Features that Power Pharmacy Workflow Efficiency*, https://www.computertalk.com/key-features-that-power-workflow-efficiency/, May/June 2020, accessed Sept.11, 2020.
Notes	

Project Title	3.5.4. Implement Finger Scanners and Medicine Label Scanners
Challenge/Wastes	Anyone performing a task in a pharmacy must be identified (legal regulation). Modern technology offers finger scanners for that purpose. The devices identify the person in a fraction of a second. Bar scanners are also used for scanning and identification of medicine labels. Without the scanners, the process is much slower and error prone.
Goals/Proposed solutions:	1. Install and implement finger scanning devices at all workstations in pharmacy. 2. Train personnel in the rigorous use of the scanners. 3. Set up alarms at the next workstation if the scan from the previous station is missing, and scan the missing one before turning the alarm off. 4. If the pharmacy has a visual control board(s) implemented, the scanners should be linked to the boards, so that the status of any order could be made visible to all staff, and upon the completion of the last task, also to waiting customers.
SoI and stakeholders	SoI: scanners at all workstations. Stakeholders: all pharmacy employees.
In-scope	Use of scanners, training of staff.
Externalities	None.
Out of scope	Design of scanners.
Major risks	Initial errors during system implementation.
Value/Expected benefits	1. Faster workflow. 2. Less waiting. 3. Higher effective capacity. 4. Fewer mistakes.

(Continued)

Literature review	Wang, B.N., Brummond, P., Stevenson, J.G. *Comparison of Barcode Scanning by Pharmacy Technicians and Pharmacists' Visual Checks for Final Product Verification*. American Journal of Health-System Pharmacy. 2016.
Notes	

Project Title	**3.5.5. Use Robots (Automated Dispensing Cabinets) for Dispensing Routine Medications**
Challenge/Wastes	Without robots, all medicines must be filled and counted manually. This causes overproduction, over-processing, defects in counting medicines, spillage, and waiting waste.
Goals/Proposed solutions:	For the most common medicines, if the long-term business case justifies it, install robots called automated dispensing cabinets that dispense and count common medicines, print the labels, and keep automatic inventory control, alarming staff to resupply the robot.
SoI and stakeholders	Robots. Pharmacy staff to be trained in the robot use.
In-scope	Robot operations.
Externalities	Pharmacy operations outside of the robots.
Out of scope	The medicines that are not placed in robots.
Major risks	1. Robot malfunction. 2. Inadequate maintenance of the robot(s)
Value/Expected benefits	Precise and fast dispensing of medicines.
Literature review	1. Goundrey-Smith, S. *Pharmacy Automation.* Information Technology in Pharmacy, 2012. 2. Chapuis, C., Roustit, M., Bal, G., Schwebel, C., Pansu, P., David-Tchouda, S., Foroni, L., Calop, J., Timsit, J., Allenet, B., Bosson, J., Bedouch, P. *Automated Drug Dispensing System Reduces Medication Errors in an Intensive Care Setting.* Critical Care Medicine, 2010.
Notes	

Project Title	3.5.6. Implement Automated Cabinets for Finished Medicine Orders Retrievable by Patient ID Number
Challenge/Wastes	Old fashion pharmacies place completed orders on shelves or countertops to wait for pick up by customers. In a busy pharmacy, this contributes to chaos and mistakes and makes finding a needed order slow and difficult. This is counterproductive for Lean workflow.
Goals/Proposed solutions:	The industry has developed efficient storage of completed prescription drugs using electronically programmable cabinets with drawers organized by patient ID number. Some cabinets offer temperature control – a highly desired feature for prolonged keeping of the medicines. The cabinets offer ease of access to a particular order, and compact use of floor space.
SoI and stakeholders	SoI: Cabinets for completed medicine orders. Stakeholders: all pharmacy employees.
In-scope	Cabinets.
Externalities	None.
Out of scope	None.
Major risks	Temperature control failure during power outage.
Value/Expected benefits	Better utilization of floor space. Easier location of the orders. Faster throughput.
	Fewer mistakes.
Literature review	Not available.
Notes	

Project Title	**3.5.7. Practice Visual Kanbans for Inventory of Medicines, Balancing Waste of Excessive Inventory with Risk of Slow Redeliveries. Implement Reminders for Medicines Requiring Refrigeration**
Challenge/Wastes	1. A typical pharmacy keeps thousands of medicines in inventory, most quite expensive. All medicines have expiration date. Lacking good Kanban system, pharmacy risks experiencing shortages of some medicines, wastage of outdated medicines, excessive and costly inventory that consumes profit margin, and risks unauthorized use of controlled substances. 2. Min-max inventory levels should be periodically reviewed and adjusted to match the average rate of consumption. 3. For minimum cost, promote just-in-time resupply system.
Goals/Proposed solutions:	1. Implement a rigorous Kanban system for all medicines in inventory, so that the amount on hand is visually displayed. Min-max inventory levels should be periodically reviewed and adjusted to match the average rate of consumption. 2. Implement signals to reorder medicines just-in-time with small buffers. 3. Implement warnings about medicines approaching the expiration date. 4. Implement warnings for medicines requiring refrigeration. 5. Keep controlled substances safely stored, with loud alarms if unauthorized use is detected. 6. The signals and alarms should be electronic but if not, old-fashioned Lean visual Kanbans should be used.

(Continued)

Sol and stakeholders	Sol: all medicines in pharmacy inventory. Stakeholders: the pharmacy staff designated to keep inventory control and reordering.
In-scope	All medicines in inventory.
Externalities	Wholesaler or central pharmacy resupplying inventory.
Out of scope	None.
Major risks	1. Excessive inventory eating up profits and wasting obsolete medicines. 2. Inadequate inventory risking delays in providing medicines and patient safety risks. 3. Wastage of spoiled medicines that failed thermal control. 4. Excessive resupply time in systems that lack just-in-time. 5. Incompetent inventory management.
Value/Expected benefits	1. Optimized inventory levels maximizing profits. 2. No waste of obsolete or spoiled medicines. 3. No unauthorized use of controlled substances. 4. Fewer mistakes. 5. Satisfied customers and pharmacy workers.
Literature review	Papalexi, M., Bamford, D., Dehe, B. *A Case Study of Kanban Implementation within the Pharmaceutical Supply Chain*. International Journal of Logistics Research and Applications, 2014.
Notes	

Project Title	3.5.8. Work with Providers to Standardize Handwritten Orders, using Agreed-Upon Safe Signal
Challenge/Wastes	In traditional systems, providers write prescriptions by hand. Providers are notorious for bad handwriting. Then a pharmacist must contact the provider for clarification, which is a source of major delays in pharmacies.
Goals/Proposed solutions:	1. As soon as possible, implement electronic prescription system (such as ePIMS), sending prescription to the pharmacy of patient's choice. 2. Where (1) is not available, train providers to use standardized phrases, capitalizations, and words on prescriptions to avoid errors. Example: HydROXyzine vs. HydraLAzine.
SoI and stakeholders	SoI: Interface between providers writing prescriptions and pharmacy.
In-scope	Prescriptions.
Externalities	Pharmacy operations.
Out of scope	Pharma industry.
Major risks	Safety risks due to errors in filling prescriptions.
Value/Expected benefits	Elimination of prescription errors.
Literature review	Dumasia, L., Harris, E., Drelichman, A. *Quality Performance Improvement with the Implementation of Standard Chemotherapy Order Forms.* Journal of Oncology Practice, 2006.
Notes	

3.6 Imaging Laboratories

Project Title	3.6.1. Schedule Imaging Tests for Maximum Capacity
Challenge/Wastes	Large imaging equipment (such as large X-ray, MRI, CT scan machines) tends to be expensive and should be utilized to maximum. Bad management of imaging laboratory causes bottlenecks, extends throughput time, and reduces effective capacity of the laboratory.
Goals/Proposed solutions:	1. Schedule patients and staff for maximum utilization of equipment and maximum availability to patients. 2. Promote continuous flow (just-in-time) of patients through the system, with minimum batching. 3. Schedule patients with minimal time gaps between tests (just enough for the current patient to move out, check and sanitize the machine, and invite the next patient, plus a short buffer for personal time). 4. Use at least three nearby small private changing rooms, say 1, 2, and 3 for each test equipment, to permit maximum utilization of the equipment. Except for the beginning and end of a test day, at any time there should be 3 patients in the lab: the patient being tested who keeps belongings in Room 1, the next patient readying in Room 2, and previous patient dressing in Room 3; and so on in rotation. 5. Schedule "routine" cases first in the day, and difficult cases (patients with mobility limitations, claustrophobia, etc.) that require more time for later in the day. 6. Verify the images in real time and repeat test if needed while the patient is still available.

(Continued)

	7. Perform maintenance and calibration during off-hours.
Sol and stakeholders	Sol: the laboratory. Patients, scheduler, staff.
In-scope	Laboratory operations and scheduling.
Externalities	Equipment maintenance and operators' training.
Out of scope	Transport of patients to and from lab.
Major risks	With tight scheduling, errors and mistakes will cause domino effect of delays and overtime.
Value/Expected benefits	1. High utilization of resources. 2. Shorter wait time by patients for lab.
Literature review	Granja, C., Almada-Lobo, B., Janela, F., Seabra, J., Mendes, A. *An Optimization based on Simulation Approach to the Patient Admission Scheduling Problem: Diagnostic Imaging Department Case Study.* Journal of Digital Imaging, 2013.
Notes	

Project Title	3.6.2. Avoid Waiting Waste in Imaging Laboratory
Challenge/Wastes	Traditional batching of patients, images, and results, as well as the lack of concurrency in the lab (inviting the new patient, waiting until undressed, prepping the patient, performing the test, waiting until the patient dresses up and leaves before inviting the next patient) dramatically slows down the system. When a test may take 20 min, with the wasteful time of undressing, dressing, waiting, and others, the cycle time doubles or triples, thus decreasing the lab utilization by the same factor. Lack of good real-time communication with transporters causes delays in patient arrival and departure times from the lab.
Goals/Proposed solutions:	1. Implement Lean workflow: invite and prep the patient, perform the test at the same time verifying correct image/file, upload to EHR, move the patient to dressing room or transport station, sanitize the equipment, and invite the next patient. The dressing and undressing should be done in separate rooms concurrently with another patient being served in the machine (see Enabler 3.6.1) 2. Invest in electronic transmittal of images and interpretations between stakeholders (ordering physician, EHR, interpreting physician(s)). 3. Operate just-in-time: send images to interpreting MD as soon as they are ready (one set of images per patient sent at once, without batching of patients) 4. Make arrangements with image readers to read and write up images as soon as they are received and upload the results to EHR

(*Continued*)

	immediately after reading, one patient at a time, without batching the patients. 5. Invest in pager-type (or uber-type) or visual boards to notify transporters when patient needs to be transported to/from lab, and communicate proactively ("patient X will be ready in x minutes")
Sol and stakeholders	Staff of the Laboratory, and image readers.
In-scope	Scheduling of patients. Reading the results.
Externalities	EHR
Out of scope	Lab equipment.
Major risks	None.
Value/Expected benefits	1. High utilization of resources. 2. Shorter wait time by patients for lab.
Literature review	Gupta, S., Kapil, S., Sharma, M. *Improvement of Laboratory Turnaround Time using Lean Methodology*. International Journal of Health Care Quality Assurance, 2018.
Notes	

Project Title	3.6.3. Close Testing Loop
Challenge/Wastes	The fragmentation between patient, provider ordering a test, the test facility, and the provider seeing and reacting to the test results is all too common, causing the "unclosed loop/dropped ball syndrome" with potentially tragic consequences for the patient.
Goals/Proposed solutions:	1. Automate test resulting to EHR system in real time. 2. Notify ordering physician when image plus interpretation are ready. Track each test from order to notification of ordering physicians and raise alarm if "dropped ball" detected after a prescribed amount of time. 3. Clearly warn physician if test is positive and assure confirmation in EHR.
SoI and stakeholders	SoI: patient, provider ordering the test, test lab, EHR.
In-scope	Every entity taking part in the test loop.
Externalities	None.
Out of scope	Other medical activities not connected to the test.
Major risks	Major safety risks to the patient if positive test result remains unread and not reacted upon in a timely manner.
Value/Expected benefits	Elimination of major dangers of fragmentation in testing: open loops.
Literature review	1. Ward B., *Close the Loop on Test Results*, Patient Safety Monitor Journal, February 18, 2020. 2. IHI, *Closing the Loop: A Guide to Safer Ambulatory Referrals in the EHR Era*, Cambridge, Massachusetts: Institute for Healthcare Improvement; 2017.
Notes	

Project Title	3.6.4. Perform Rigorous Scheduled Maintenance of Lab Equipment to Avoid Unscheduled Downtime
Challenge/Wastes	For convenience of maintenance crew, all lab equipment is stopped, and maintenance performed during normal operating hours, thus reducing lab utilization and causing delays in patient tests, diagnoses, and treatments.
Goals/Proposed solutions:	1. Perform scheduled maintenance during off-hours only. 2. Perform all maintenance required by equipment manufacturers to avoid breakdowns and unscheduled downtime. 3. If the equipment breaks down, call and schedule repairs immediately, and make arrangements with repair vendors to be available in a short time.
Sol and stakeholders	The given machine, maintenance crew, technicians operating the equipment, and patients waiting for the test.
In-scope	Factory-required equipment maintenance. Also repairs.
Externalities	Equipment manufacturer.
Out of scope	Training in equipment use.
Major risks	Potentially higher rates for equipment maintenance during off-hours.
Value/Expected benefits	Avoidance of scheduled or unscheduled maintenance downtime during lab operating hours. Maximization of equipment utilization.
Literature review	Poulter, B. *Ways to Help Eliminate Unscheduled Downtime, Dassault Systems*, February 4, 2015.
Notes	

Project Title	3.6.5. Avoid Motion and Transportation Waste
Challenge/Wastes	The clinics and hospitals (including EDs and ORs) that lack portable (on carts) radiology equipment (small x-ray, ultrasound, EKG, etc.) need to transport the patient needing the image to the imaging laboratory, transporting the patient both ways. This is inconvenient and risky to the patient, and introduces motion and transportation waste, time delays, overproduction, and over-processing wastes.
Goals/Proposed solutions:	1. Invest in portable radiology equipment for quick bedside use where applicable. 2. Promote continuous flow (just-in-time) of patients through the system, with minimum batching. 3. Locate stationary radiology equipment near the ED/hospital for shortest transport time of patients, where feasible. 4. Eliminate long wasteful walks throughout building corridors or between buildings. 5. Use visual controls to provide information on the status and flow of laboratory. The information should be accessible remotely.
Sol and stakeholders	Patient, providers ordering the test, portable test equipment.
In-scope	Portable test equipment.
Externalities	Imaging laboratory.
Out of scope	Major equipment in imaging laboratory.
Major risks	Balancing business case between the cost of portable equipment and cost of training of providers versus the cost of waste of transporting the patient to imaging laboratory.

(*Continued*)

Value/Expected benefits	Faster (more just-in-time) testing of patient at bedside, conducive to faster diagnosis and treatment, and avoidance of delays and transportation costs.
Literature review	Andrea, C. *Waste Savings in Patient Transportation Inside Large Hospitals Using Lean Thinking Tools and Logistic Solutions.* Leadership in Health Services, 2013.
Notes	

Project Title	3.6.6. Avoid Over-Processing Waste of Ordering Unnecessary Tests
Challenge/Wastes	In the United States, a massive number of tests of all kinds are prescribed every year, many of which are medically unnecessary, driven by pursuit of revenue and avoidance of legal exposure.
Goals/Proposed solutions:	1. Avoid inappropriate or medically unnecessary diagnostic tests. 2. Implement checks in EHR system to flag such orders, asking the provider to confirm the need for the test. 3. Collect statistics of test orders for subsequent discussions and corrective actions at department level.
Sol and stakeholders	All providers ordering tests, and all tests ordered.
In-scope	All providers ordering tests, and all tests ordered.
Externalities	None.
Out of scope	None
Major risks	Intimidated providers may cause under-use of tests even in medically justified situations.
Value/Expected benefits	1. Cost savings from unnecessary tests to patients and payers, and lesser burden on test equipment. 2. Time savings in diagnosis and treatment. 3. Health savings from fewer tests that carry health risks (e.g. radiation).
Literature review	Kaiser Health News, *Unnecessary Medical Tests, Treatments Cost $200 Billion Annually, Cause Harm*, Kaiser Health News, May 2, 2017.
Notes	

Project Title	3.6.7. Avoid Inventory Waste
Challenge/Wastes	Inventory (batching) waste causes significant delays in the system and lowers the utilization of test resources
Goals/Proposed solutions:	1. Do not batch cases, patients, test interpretations. Instead, test, send for interpretation, read and interpret, and send the result back to EHR just-in-time using "single piece flow," one patient at a time. 2. Process STAT (urgent) tests in the order they came, unless "critical" has higher priority (e.g., the opened patient is waiting on OR table). 3. Standardize test supplies and inventory levels on hand to avoid shortages and excessive inventory waste.
SoI and stakeholders	All tests, all patients, all providers ordering or reading tests in the system.
In-scope	All tests, all patients, all providers ordering or reading tests in the system.
Externalities	None.
Out of scope	None.
Major risks	None.
Value/Expected benefits	Time savings in diagnosis and treatment.
	Health savings from fewer tests that carry health risks (e.g. radiation).
Literature review	Rodney, H., *An Exploration of Healthcare Inventory and Lean Management in Minimizing Medical Supply Waste in Healthcare Organizations.* Walden University – ProQuest Dissertations Publishing, 2013.
Notes	

3.7 Clinical Laboratories

Project Title	3.7.1 Avoid Errors in Phlebotomy and Sample Collection
Challenge/Wastes	1. Mistakes in sample collection are costly to remedy (the patient must be contacted and asked to return for phlebotomy), delay the test and diagnosis, and risk deterioration of patient condition. 2. Mistakes occur because a sample is placed in a wrong container; container cap comes off spilling the sample (and potentially contaminating the entire phlebotomy station and affected lab areas); a sample is not registered properly into the system scanner, label is not printed properly or is missing; vials are piled up randomly which requires lengthy manual sorting; and some may spill from the container and be lost.
Goals/Proposed solutions:	1. Improve the system to avoid errors in sample collection with proper training, visual aids, and space organization. 2. Mark phlebotomy vials with different standardized color caps for different test types. 3. Prepare and display posters in phlebotomy stations showing vial types visually. 4. Sort vials into bins in real time right at the phlebotomy station, and place vials vertically into holders for safer transport and easier sorting in lab. 5. Carefully verify patient ID and verify that the label is printed well and is well attached to the container.

(Continued)

Sol and stakeholders	Sol: Phlebotomy stations. Stakeholders: patients, phlebotomists.
In-scope	Collection and registration of samples.
Externalities	Transport of samples to the lab.
Out of scope	Lab activities.
Major risks	If no improvement undertaken, continued errors and failures of phlebotomy.
Value/Expected benefits	1. Elimination of errors in phlebotomy. 2. Savings in time and cost. 3. Faster diagnosis.
Literature review	1. Rana S.V., *No Preanalytical Errors in Laboratory Testing: A Beneficial Aspect for Patients.* Indian Journal of Clinical Biochemistry, 2012. 2. Lippi, G., Chance, J.J., Church, S., et al. *Preanalytical Quality Improvement: From Dream to Reality.* Clinical Chemistry and Laboratory Medicine. 2011. 3. Salinas, M., Lopez-Garrigos, M., Flores, E., Gutiérrez, M., Lugo, J., Uris, J. *Three Years of Preanalytical Errors: Quality Specifications and Improvement through Implementation of Statistical Process Control.* Scandinavian Journal of Clinical and Laboratory Investigation, 2009.
Notes	

Project Title	3.7.2. Transport Samples Efficiently to Remote Laboratory
Challenge/Wastes	1. Some transportation systems collecting samples and transporting them to a central clinical laboratory are organized inefficiently. Usually this is an outgrowth of ad-hoc planning and adding medical centers and routes. Inefficient organization causes delays in sample delivery time to the lab, and inefficient use of transportation infrastructure: trucks and drivers. 2. Often, expensive drivers are asked to walk the maze of corridors to pick up samples, while the expensive truck is idle. 3. Drivers are often sent on errands that have no relation to the sample transportation. 4. Driving times are poorly synchronized to traffic conditions and the city routing.
Goals/Proposed solutions:	1. Implement efficient city/regional transport of samples by dividing the routes into synchronized local and long-distance routes, with each optimized for minimum time. The local routes should be cyclic taking 1–2 hours each even in traffic, picking up samples from several nearby sites and delivering them to the long-distance trucks for transfer to the lab at predetermined times (perhaps hourly or every two hours, or so). The time of drivers (and trucks sitting idle) should not be wasted waiting for the driver to walk the maze of the medical center picking up samples. Instead, the samples should be delivered in tots periodically to the local truck pick up station by local employees. The timing of these deliveries should be synchronized with truck schedules. This system will guarantee that the longest transport time of

(Continued)

	a sample from any location is the cycle time of the local truck, plus the cycle time of the long-distance truck. 2. Do not give the trucks intended for sample transportation any other responsibility (mail, packages, errands) and limit their work to transportation of samples. Designate a few trucks and drivers in the system for extra errands and commit the remaining trucks and drivers to the task of transporting samples to the central lab. 3. Practice minimum batch size and optimize for shortest test turnaround time. 4. Use google maps or equivalent tool to optimize the routes in traffic in real time.
SoI and stakeholders	SoI: transportation trucks and drivers used to carry samples from local medical centers to a central laboratory.
In-scope	Timing and routes of trucks, responsibilities of the drivers.
Externalities	Hand carrying of samples from local phlebotomy stations to the sample pick up location by local trucks.
Out of scope	Errands other than sample transportation.
Major risks	Resistance from some drivers whose routes would change, affecting previous personal convenience (e.g. pick up of children from school).

(Continued)

Value/Expected benefits	1. Typically, vastly more efficient transportation system, with shorter test throughput times, conducive to faster diagnosis. 2. Better utilization of transportation infrastructure.
Literature review	Oppenheim, B.W., Kanter, M.H., Bueno, O., Dizon, L.D., Farnacio, L.M., Medina, P.L., Moradian, M. M., Tabata, C., Tiffert, M.S., *Lean Enablers for Clinical Laboratories*. Research in Medical & Engineering Sciences, November 27, 2017
Notes	

Project Title	3.7.3. Practice Smallest Batches and Continuous Flow of Samples throughout the System
Challenge/Wastes	Batching of samples throughout the clinical laboratory system all the way across from phlebotomy to resulting in EHR is notorious. Yet, it is destructive to efficiency, extends the throughput time, decreases system utilization, is prone to errors and defects, and has long been known as a disaster of "mass production." The entire system should strive to make the batches as small as possible, and to move them to the next step as soon as possible. Batching is often excused by the use of reagents, or maintenance needs, or work shifts, or having to wait for resulting, or discreet transportation needs, and others. None of these excuses is valid and literature exists to debunk all these arguments.
Goals/Proposed solutions:	1. Keep optimizing the flow of samples by minimizing batch sizes and promoting continuous flow from collection, through transport, sorting in laboratory, loading samples into analyzer machines, and resulting. 2. Do not perform maintenance and calibration on all machines at once as this stops the flow. Perform maintenance and calibration on one machine at a time while other machines work. 3. Avoid batching of samples in storage for the next day.
SoI and stakeholders	SoI: entire value flow from sample collection to resulting for all samples, all collection sites, entire transport system, and laboratory operations.
In-scope	Entire value flow.
Externalities	None.
Out of scope	None.

(Continued)

Major risks	None.
Value/Expected benefits	1. Faster throughput of tests. 2. Better utilization of expensive resources. 3. Less waste in the entire system. 4. Faster diagnosis and better care for patients. 5. Better traceability of samples.
Literature review	Oppenheim, B.W., Kanter, M.H., Bueno, O., Dizon, L.D., Farnacio, L.M., Medina, P.L., Moradian, M. M., Tabata, C., Tiffert, M.S., *Lean Enablers for Clinical Laboratories*. Research in Medical & Engineering Sciences, November 27, 2017.
Notes	

Project Title	3.7.4. Eliminate Non-Value Adding Tasks Such As Tedious Manual Transfer of Samples from Sample Collection Vials to Analyzing Instrument Tubes. Instead Distribute the Instrument Tubes to Phlebotomists to Fill at the Phlebotomy Stations and Transport them in Sanitary Trays that Can Be Inserted Directly into the Analyzers.
Challenge/Wastes	One of the most wasteful activities in the value chain of clinical testing is the manual transfer (pouring) of samples from collection vials to the tubes used in the analyzing instruments. One large national lab has to do it 15 million times every year. This is a grotesque waste of human resources. The transfer is also conducive to spillage (dangerous during pandemics and when dealing with other infected samples), lost samples, and breakage.
Goals/Proposed solutions:	Eliminate the manual transfer of samples altogether. Distribute the instrument tubes to phlebotomists to fill at the phlebotomy stations and transport them in sanitized trays that can be inserted directly into the analyzers.
Sol and stakeholders	Manufacturers of tubes. Handlers of samples. Phlebotomists. Instrument operators.
In-scope	All sample containers that require manual transfer from one container type to another.
Externalities	None.
Out of scope	The samples which do not require manual transfer.
Major risks	Resistance from the individuals performing the transfer and unions.

(Continued)

Value/Expected benefits	1. Savings of labor, cost, and test throughput time. 2. Less risk of breakage, spillage, contamination.
Literature review	Oppenheim, B.W., Kanter, M.H., Bueno, O., Dizon, L.D., Farnacio, L.M., Medina, P.L., Moradian, M. M., Tabata, C., Tiffert, M.S., *Lean Enablers for Clinical Laboratories*. Research in Medical & Engineering Sciences, November 27, 2017.
Notes	

Project Title	3.7.5. For Non-24-Hour Operations, Stagger Staff to Complete and Result Tests on the Same Day as When the Sample Arrived at the Lab.
Challenge/Wastes	After the sample has been analyzed by an instrument, it often must be manually evaluated and resulted by a clinical technician or an MD/PhD. At the beginning of the first shift, the technician has no samples to evaluate as they are not ready yet, and at the end of the shift, or second shift, samples are still coming out of the instrument, but time has run out to result them. In consequence, a portion of the samples are resulted the next day. This delays the diagnosis and is detrimental to good care.
Goals/Proposed solutions:	Stagger the hours of the evaluating and resulting staff relative to the hours of the laboratory by a few hours (start late and end late), so that all samples analyzed in each day can be evaluated and resulted on the same day. This reduces the test turnaround time and is conducive to faster diagnosis.
Sol and stakeholders	The staff resulting the tests.
In-scope	The staff.
Externalities	None.
Out of scope	None.
Major risks	None.
Value/Expected benefits	1. All samples analyzed in each day can be evaluated and resulted on the same day. 2. Shorter test turnaround time and faster diagnosis of patients.
Literature review	Oppenheim, B.W., Kanter, M.H., Bueno, O., Dizon, L.D., Farnacio, L.M., Medina, P.L., Moradian, M. M., Tabata, C., Tiffert, M.S., *Lean Enablers for Clinical Laboratories*, Research in Medical & Engineering Sciences, November 27, 2017.
Notes	

Project Title	3.7.6. Rearchitect Lab Spaces to Minimize Walking and Transport of Samples, Supplies, and Materials
Challenge/Wastes	Some clinical laboratories have inefficient layout which forces the staff to do lots of walking and transporting supplies and samples between workstations. This is particularly true in the labs that grew the test volume, never stopping to streamline operations.
Goals/Proposed solutions:	Rearchitect lab spaces to arrange the workflow into sequential work stations arranged in the order of use, with the last station close to the first. This is conducive to lean flow of samples and supplies, and minimizes the motion and transportation waste, as well as waiting waste. First, prepare a good consensus-based plan. Then rearchitect a part of the lab at a time so as not to disrupt the lab operations, best during off-hours.
SoI and stakeholders	SoI: the laboratory. Stakeholders: all employees of the laboratory.
In-scope	All activities in the lab.
Externalities	None.
Out of scope	None.
Major risks	Test disruption during the change from old layout to new.
Value/Expected benefits	1. Optimized Lean flow of the work. 2. Reduction of motion, transportation, and waiting waste. 3. Faster test turnround time. 4. Better work environment. 5. Faster diagnosis of patients.

(Continued)

Literature review	Oppenheim, B.W., Kanter, M.H., Bueno, O., Dizon, L.D., Farnacio, L.M., Medina, P.L., Moradian, M. M., Tabata, C., Tiffert, M.S., *Lean Enablers for Clinical Laboratories*. Research in Medical & Engineering Sciences, November 27, 2017.
Notes	

3.8 Population Health

Project Title	**3.8.1 Increase Wellness and Improve Chronic Care using KP-Like "Complete Care" [Kanter, 2013] for Pre-Visit, during Visit, After Visit**
Challenge/Wastes	Huge populations of patients have their morbidities cared for one at a time, mostly during personal visits to clinics.
Goals/Proposed solutions:	1. Computer technology and internet has enabled dramatic progress in population care. Kaiser Permanente team [Kanter, 2013] has created a general framework and template and used it to expand chronic care and wellness for managing a large number of illnesses/morbidities (26 at recent count), e.g., A1C, hypertension, colorectal tests, cervical-breast tests, medication adherence, asthma, etc. In each case the approach is to display to providers the pre-visit information (capturing the health information, and informing how the patient and providers are to prepare for the visit), during-visit information (comprehensively checking health parameters, tests/treatments and vaccinations due, medication updates, etc.), and after-visit follow up which is consistent with the given advanced population care knowledge. 2. Once the general framework has been successfully created and validated, it can be extended to new chronic illnesses and wellness treatments, one at a time. 3. Include additional care gaps in proactive office encounter checklists; these relate to elder care, advance directives, posthospital care, immunizations, health maintenance, and pregnancy care.

(Continued)

Sol and stakeholders	The entire population of patients.
In-scope	The illnesses/morbidities addressed.
Externalities	Patients outside of the institution.
Out of scope	None.
Major risks	Success of the method for several population illnesses risks complacency and relaxed verification and validation when expanding the method to a new illness/morbidity.
Value/Expected benefits	Extraordinary improvement in care of a large number of patients, which would be impossible without the population health approach.
Literature review	Kanter, M., Lindsay, G., Bellows, J. *Complete Care at Kaiser Permanente: Transforming Chronic and Preventative Care.* Joint Commission Journal on Quality and Patient Safety, 2013.
Notes	

Project Title	3.8.2 Design a High-Capacity Field Facility for High-Fidelity Testing of Virus during Pandemic
Challenge/Wastes	As the recent COVID-19 pandemic demonstrated, the national high-fidelity infection test capacity was too small by several orders of magnitude. In many countries some poorer than the U.S., capacity was created very fast to test practically 100% of population using fast-erected dedicated field laboratories. In the United States,the wait for test results by major clinical laboratories is often 5-10 days, which is useless for contact tracing and preventive measures. Given that the sum of value-adding activities in a test is measured in minutes (sample collection and patient ID capture 2 min), transport to the testing instrument and sample preparation (15 min), analysis in the instrument (30 min on a fast machine), resulting to the database (seconds), electronic notification of the patient (seconds), for one test a one-hour turnaround should be the goal. The massive delays and slow turnaround times are the result of batching tests and remote locations of test sites, so that transportation to the lab and waiting consume almost all the time. There is a way to do it vastly better.
Goals/Proposed solutions:	Create a field test facility on any large and reasonably clean parking lot available. Ask military to sanitize the asphalt and erect a large tent.
	Divide the tent into four rooms: 1. The first room, with no walls, is the drive-thru or walk-thru for patients, with two stops: registration of the patient, and sample collection. The registration station should be operated by computer technicians using laptops and entering each patient ID and

(Continued)

answers to a few health questions. The laptops are to be connected wirelessly to the resulting server in the last room of the tent (see below). After giving the sample the patient is free to leave. Create as many pairs of registration + collection stations in parallel as needed to match the needed flow. Have room to add more such station pairs, if needed. The patient will be notified by email or text of the test results, plus instructions for follow up if the test is positive. Collect the samples into a tray of 10 samples, and manually carry the tray to the next room for analysis. A small sanitized room adjacent to the collection room should be used for inventory of sample collection kits.

2. Install the needed analyzer instruments in the second room (start with 10 instruments laid out in parallel, and have room to add more instruments later, if needed). Provide power to the machines from a nearest power source or from a generator. National guards should be helping with this task. This room should be under overpressure for sanitation purposes. Operate the instruments in parallel. Perform scheduled maintenance one machine at a time. In the instrument room have storage for supplies and reagents. Have a logistical expert (best from military) work to assure the just-in-time delivery of supplies and reagents, and the delivery and installation of the instruments. Demand fast delivery (fastest possible transportation time plus small reserve).

3. Install a server in the third room. Connect the instruments electronically to the server for

(Continued)

	automatic uploading of the results, notifying the patient, and updating the database for follow up.
	4. Room 4 should serve the personnel: storage of PPE supplies, enclosed bins for biological waste, enclosed area with portable toilets, enclosed sanitized area for food self-service: microwaves, coffee machines, refrigerators.
	Organize the flow as a Lean flow, registering the patient and collecting the sample, loading the sample into a small tray (batch) that can be loaded directly into the machine, carrying trays to the next available analyzer, removing the tray for cleaning while the machine results the tests, and starting again at the beginning, in a 24/7 continuous just-in-time single-piece flow system, with the tray being "a piece." This work organization assures maximum capacity, fast flow, and shortest possible turnaround time.
SoI and stakeholders	Field test facility. All workers preparing and operating the facility.
In-scope	All activities of setting up and operating the facility: 1. Military staff to erect the tent and install power and instruments. 2. Logistics staff to organize delivery of instruments, generator, supplies, reagents, test kits, PPE supplies, waste bins, and organize disposal 3. Electronics technician to install laptops and server and prepare software. 4. Instrument technicians to operate the analyzing instruments. 5. Negotiations with vendors, military and local governments.

(Continued)

Externalities	Activities outside of the test tent.
Out of scope	Financing of the test facility – should be left up to the local government.
Major risks	Lack of needed items. Alternative sourcing should then be pursued.
Value/Expected benefits	A field test facility with capacity of 50,000 tests per day can be set up in one week. Expanding the capacity by another 50,000 tests per day can be accomplished in much shorter time.
Literature review	Flexx, https://www.flexxproductions.com/news/hospital-field-tents-and-medical-testing-tents-from-flexx-productions/, accessed Sept. 11, 2020.
Notes	

Project Title	3.8.3 Reduce Disparity in Vaccination Rates between White and Minority Populations
Challenge/Wastes	Because of dramatic historical events (e.g., Tuskagee syphilis experiments on African Americans), there is a significant distrust of vaccinations in the community. The rates are significantly below those of the Whites.
Goals/Proposed solutions:	1. Initiate steps to reduce disparity in vaccination rates between White and Minority Populations. 2. Use all patient visits in any clinic in the system as an opportunity to educate the patient and deliver vaccination on the spot. Debunk conspiracy theories about "harmful health effects." 3. Distribute flyers about the vaccinations to the entire population of member patients. 4. Invite patients to watch educational videos, attend educational events delivered by minority nurses. 5. Work with community centers (e.g., churches, schools, sports groups) to invite minority nurses to offer a teach-in about vaccinations and administer vaccinations on the spot. 6. Make vaccination process easy via drive-ins. 7. Work with local TV channels to promote vaccinations.
Sol and stakeholders	All member patients of the medical organization. Community. Clinics, churches, schools, sports.
In-scope	See "Goals" above.
Externalities	NA
Out of scope	NA

(Continued)

Major risks	Lack of success. Keep trying different approaches and do not give up if lack of sucecss is observed in a given iteration.
Value/Expected benefits	Higher vaccination rates. Better health of the entire population. Less economic losses from illnesses.
Literature review	1. Lu, P., O'Halloran, A., Williams, W.W., Lindley, M.C., Farrall, S., Bridges, C.B.B. *Racial and Ethnic Disparities in Vaccination Coverage among Adult Population.* American Journal of Preventive Medicine, 2015. 2. Pattin, A.J., *Disparities in the Use of Immunization Services Among Underserved Minority Patient Populations and the Role of Pharmacy Technicians: A Review.* Journal of Pharmacy Technology, 2017.
Notes	

Project Title	3.8.4 Improve Vaccination Rates for COVID-19, Flu, and Other Routine Shots
Challenge/Wastes	Two different but somewhat overlapping situations prevent massive acceptance of flu/standard vaccinations and COVID-19 vaccinations. Because of trashy internet sites promoting conspiracy theories against vaccinations (e.g., "flu vaccine causes autism"), a significant portion of society is opposed to flu and other standard vaccinations. Regarding COVID-19 vaccine, some individuals do not trust the "warp speed development of vaccination" and prefer to wait and see how effective and how safe the vaccination is.
Goals/Proposed solutions:	1. Create a massive ongoing educational campaign in mass media, both social networks and traditional (TV, newspapers). Being a public health issue, it should be paid for by federal and state governments. It should be produced by marketing experts and community leaders using trusted health experts in promotions. 2. Education by nurses in all visits to clinics. 3. Education in K-12 and higher education schools. 4. School boards should forbid entry of a child into school who has not been vaccinated. 5. Campaign in social gatherings (e.g., churches). 6. For COVID-19, airlines should make ticket sale conditional on proof of vaccination. 7. DMV should require proof of vaccination when requesting or renewing DL. 8. Employers should demand proof of vaccination as a condition of continued employment.
Sol and stakeholders	The entire society.
In-scope	All individuals who have not been vaccinated yet.

(Continued)

Externalities	None.
Out of scope	Individuals already vaccinated.
Major risks	Resistance from fringe groups of society complaining about "the lack of freedom" and "big brother."
Value/Expected benefits	1. Eradication of debilitating and deadly illnesses, including COVID-19. 2. Revival of economy.
Literature review	1. Chen, F., Stevens, R. *Applying Lessons from Behavioral Economics to Increase Flu Vaccination Rates.* Health Promotion International, 2017. 2. Dexter, L.J., Teare, M.D., Dexter, M., Siriwardena, A.N., Read, R.C. *Strategies to Increase Influenza Vaccination Rates: Outcomes of a Nationwide Cross-Sectional Survey of UK General Practice.* BMJ Open, 2012.
Notes	

Project Title	3.8.5 Implement Remote Blood Pressure Monitoring and Automated Uploads of Data to EHR
Challenge/Wastes	The patients suffering from hypertension need frequent monitoring of blood pressure. Using traditional device is inconvenient, and patients must remember to manually upload the current measurement into the EHR application. Because it is inconvenient, it is not done as often as it should be, creating health risks.
Goals/Proposed solutions:	1. Modern automatic devices are capable of automatic measurements and automatic uploading to the EHR, making the device highly convenient and reliable. 2. Patients must be persuaded to wear the monitor and learn how to use it. 3. A strong population health initiative should be conducted inviting the patient to participate. 4. Every contact with any provider in the system should reinforce the invitation and inform of the benefits. 5. Emails and flyers should be distributed to the applicable patients.
SoI and stakeholders	SoI: The patients needing remote blood pressure monitors. The providers involved in patient education in the benefits and use of the device.
In-scope	Blood pressure monitoring.
Externalities	Design of the device.
Out of scope	Monitoring of other vitals.
Major risks	Psychological resistance from some patients who are suspicious of "big brother spying."

(Continued)

Value/Expected benefits	1. Systematic and reliable monitoring of blood pressure. 2. Ability to immediately respond to the patient by texting that the current reading is too high, and the patient must undertake a suggested action. 3. Healthier patients, fewer heart attacks and strokes.
Literature review	1. Safavi, K.C., Driscoll, W., Wiener-Kronish, J.P., *Remote Surveillance Technologies: Realizing the Aim of Right Patient, Right Data, Right Time.* Anesthesia and Analgesia, 2018. 2. Genes, N., Violante, S., Cetrangol, C., Rogers, L., Schadt, E.E., Chan, Y.Y.C. *From Smartphone to EHR: A Case Report on Integrating Patient-Generated Health Data.* Nature. June 2018.
Notes	

Project Title	3.8.6 Implement Remote Glucose Monitoring and Automated Uploads of Data to EHR
Challenge/Wastes	The diabetic patients need frequent monitoring of the glucose level. Using traditional device is inconvenient, and patients must remember to manually upload the current measurement into the EHR application. Because it is inconvenient, it is not done as often as it should be, creating health risks.
Goals/Proposed solutions:	1. Modern automatic devices are capable of automatic measurements and automatic uploading to the EHR, making the device highly convenient and reliable. 2. Patients must be persuaded to wear the monitor and learn how to use it. 3. A strong population health initiative should be conducted inviting the patient to participate. 4. Every contact with any provider in the system should reinforce the invitation and inform of the benefits. 5. Emails and flyers should be distributed to the applicable patients.
SoI and stakeholders	SoI: The patients needing remote glucose monitors. The providers involved in patient education in the benefits and use of the device.
In-scope	Glucose monitoring.
Externalities	Design of the device.
Out of scope	Monitoring of other vitals.
Major risks	Psychological resistance from some patients who are suspicious of "big brother spying."
Value/Expected benefits	1. Systematic and reliable monitoring of glucose.

(Continued)

	2. Ability to immediately respond to the patient by texting that the current reading is too high, and the patient must undertake a suggested action. 3. Healthier patients, fewer complications from diabetes.
Literature review	1. Espinoza, J., Shah, P., Raymond, J. *Integrating Continuous Glucose Monitor Data Directly into the Electronic Health Record: Proof of Concept.* Diabetes Technology and Therapeutics, July 2020. 2. Benhamou, P.Y. *Improving Diabetes Management with Electronic Health Records and Patients' Health Records.* Diabetes and Metabolism, December 2011.
Note	

Project Title	**3.8.7 Implement Self-Used Apps for Mental Health and Distribute to Patients to Improve Population Health**
Challenge/Wastes	In many medical institutions, mental health patients cannot be seen by a provider as often as some would like, and the inability to see a provider when wanted is often detrimental to patient well-being, extending anxiety and potentially leading to more serious conditions.
Goals/Proposed solutions:	Distribute one or more of the apps that recently became available, such as Calm or My Strength to mental health patients free of charge, allowing the patients to stabilize their condition using yoga, mindfulness thinking, and relaxation, as guided by the app. Some apps can and should be customized based on intake interviews.
SoI and stakeholders	The population of mental health patients who are suitable for using self-apps.
In-scope	The apps approved for use by the institution.
Externalities	App vendors.
Out of scope	The apps not approved for use by the institution.
Major risks	1. Possible misuse of the app by some patients.
Value/Expected benefits	1. Ability by patients to stabilize their condition using yoga, mindfulness thinking, and relaxation, as guided by the app. 2. Less demand for face-to-face visits.
Literature review	1. Bakker, D., Kazantzis, N., Rickwood, D., Rickard, N. *A Randomized Controlled Trial of Three Smartphone Apps for Enhancing Public Mental Health*. Behaviour Research and Therapy. 2018

(Continued)

2. Donker, T., Petrie, K., Proudfoot, J., Clarke, J., Birch, M.R., Christensen, H. *Smartphones for Smarter Delivery of Mental Health Programs: A Systematic Review.* Journal of Medical Internet Research. 2013.
3. Payne, H.E., Lister, C., West, J.H., Bernhardt, J.M. *Behavioral Functionality of Mobile Apps in Health Interventions: A Systematic Review of the Literature.* JMIR Mhealth Uhealth. 2015.

Notes	

Project Title	3.8.8 Implement Mail-Order Pharmacy and Create a Network of Cooperating Pharmacies
Challenge/Wastes	1. The need to walk to a physical pharmacy to fill prescriptions in person is a major inconvenience to many patients. 2. A random collection of pharmacies used by patients makes prescription writing risky: providers write the prescription by hand, patients take them to a preferred pharmacy to fill, risking errors.
Goals/Proposed solutions:	1. Organize own or enter into a contract with an existing pharmacy to provide efficient, fast-turnaround (max 24 hrs) mail service. Negotiate for discounted prices due to volume. 2. Implement ePIMS or similar software for electronic transmittal of prescriptions. 3. Demand of all cooperating pharmacies to implement ePIMS software. 4. Invite existing pharmacies in the region to enlist for electronic transmittal of prescriptions. 5. Electronic prescriptions minimize errors from hand-written prescriptions.
Sol and stakeholders	Sol: all cooperating pharmacies, EPIMS software. Stakeholders: patients, providers, pharmacy managers.
In-scope	Pharmacies in the network.
Externalities	Management of the pharmacies.
Out of scope	Pharmacies out of network.
Major risks	None.
Value/Expected benefits	1. Convenience to patients: mail delivery of prescriptions to patient home. 2. Fewer errors from writing/reading prescriptions by hand.

(Continued)

Literature review	Kappenman, A.M., Ragsdale, R., Rim, M.H., Tyler, L.S., Nickman, N.A., *Implementation of a Centralized Mail-Order Pharmacy Service.* American Journal of Health-system Pharmacy: AJHP: Official Journal of the American Society of Health-system Pharmacists, September 2019.
Notes	

References

Al-Araidah, O., Momani, A., Khasawneh, M., Momani, M. *Lead-Time Reduction Utilizing Lean Tools Applied to Healthcare: The Inpatient Pharmacy at a Local Hospital.* Journal for Healthcare Quality, Vol. 32. No. 1, 59–66, Jan-Feb 2010.

Albrecht, U., Behrends, M., Matthies, H.K., Jan, U.V. Usage of Multilingual Mobile Translation Applications in Clinical Settings. JMIR Mhealth Uhealth, 2013 Apr 23;1(1):e4.

Algauer, A., Rivera, S., Faurote, R. *Patient-Centered Care Transition for Patients Admitted through the ED: Improving Patient and Employee Experience.* Journal of Patient Experience, Vol. 2. No. 1, 25–28, May 2015.

Andrea, C. *Waste Savings in Patient Transportation Inside Large Hospitals using Lean Thinking Tools and Logistic Solutions.* Leadership in Health Services, 10.1108/LHS-05-2012-0013.

Ansell, D., Crispo, J.A.G., Simard, B. et al. *Interventions to Reduce Wait Times for Primary Care Appointments: A Systematic Review.* BMC Health Services Research, Vol 17, pg 295, 2017.

Balch, H. The Front Line: Think Outside the Tray and Make the Most of Your Sterile Processing Career, Ultra Clean Systems, Incorporated, 2020.

Bakker, D., Kazantzis, N., Rickwood, D., Rickard, N. *A Randomized Controlled Trial of Three Smartphone Apps for Enhancing Public Mental Health.* Behaviour Research and Therapy, 2018 Oct;109:75–83.

Balestracci, D. Data Sanity: A Quantum Leap to Unprecedented Results, 2nd Edition, MGMA, 2015.

Benhamou, P.Y. *Improving Diabetes Management with Electronic Health Records and Patients' Health Records.* Diabetes and Metabolism, 2011 Dec;37 Suppl 4:S53–6.

Berry, L.L., Rock, B.L., Houskamp, B.S., Brueggeman, J., Tucker, L. *Care Coordination for Patients with Complex Health Profiles in Inpatient and Outpatient Settings.* May Foundation for Medical Education and Research, February 2013.

Bresnick, J. *Patient Navigators Shave Hours from Hospital Discharge Times; Patient Navigators May be the Key to Reducing Hospital Discharge Times and Preventing Admissions Traffic Jams,* Health IT Analytics, June 30, 2016.

Brandenburg, L., Gabow, P., Steele, G., Toussaint, J., Tyson, B. *Innovation and Best Practices in Health Care Scheduling.* Institute of Medicine of the National Academies, 2015.

Bresnick, J. *Patient Navigators Shave Hours from Hospital Discharge Times; Patient Navigators May Be the Key to Reducing Hospital Discharge Times and Preventing Admissions Traffic Jams.* Health IT Analytics, June 30, 2016.

Brown, F. SELP Director, Loyola Marymount University, Los Angeles, private communication with the author, 2009.

Byczkowski, M. *Collaborating for a Better Tomorrow: The Operating Room of the Future,* www.digitalistmagazine.com, accessed Sept. 11, 2020.

Carter, A.B. The Under Secretary of Defense, Acquisition, Technology and Logistics, Memorandum for Acquisition Professionals, June 28, 2010.

Carter, N., Valaitis, R.K., Lam, A., Feather, J., Nicholl, J., Cleghorn, L. *Navigation Delivery Models and Roles of Navigators in Primary Care: A Scoping Literature Review.* BMC Health Services Research, Vol. 18, pg 96, 2018.

Charnow, C., Modi, P., Sage, A., Staton, M. Analysis of the Instrument Picking Process in a Case Cart System at the University of Michigan Hospital, University of Michigan Health System: Program and Operations Analysis, 2010.

Caesar, U., Karlsson, J., Olsson, L., Samuelsson, K., Hannsson-Olofsson, E. *Incidence and Root Causes of Cancellations for Elective Orthopaedic Procedures: A Single Center Experience of 17,625 Consecutive Cases.* Patient Safety in Surgery, 2014.

Chen, F., Stevens, R. *Applying Lessons from Behavioral Economics to Increase Flu Vaccination Rates.* Health Promotion International, 2017.

Chenoweth, D.H., Garrett, J. *Cost-Effectiveness Analysis of a Worksite Clinic.* American Association of Occupational Health Nurses, Vol. 54. No. 2, February 2006.

Chowdhury, D., Duggal, A.K. *Intensive Care Unit Models: Do You Want Them to Be Open Or Closed? A Critical Review.* Neurol India, 2017.

Chapuis, C., Roustit, M., Bal, G., Schwebel, C., Pansu, P., David-Tchouda, S., Foroni, L., Calop, J., Timsit, J., Allenet, B., Bosson, J., Bedouch, P. *Automated Drug Dispensing System Reduces Medication Errors in an Intensive Care Setting.* Critical Care Medicine, 2010.

Clausing, D. Total Quality Development: A Step - By - Step Guide to World – Class Concurrent Engineering, ASME Press, New York, 1994.

Computertalk, *Key Features that Power Pharmacy Workflow Efficiency,* https://www.computertalk.com/key-features-that-power-workflow-efficiency/, May/June 2020, accessed Sept.11, 2020.

Dexter, L.J., Teare, M.D., Dexter, M., Siriwardena, A.N., Read, R.C. *Strategies to Increase Influenza Vaccination Rates: Outcomes of a Nationwide Cross-Sectional Survey of UK General Practice.* BMJ Open, 2012.

DODAF (Architecture Framework), V2.0, May 28, 2009.

Dodds, S. R. *Systems Engineering in Healthcare – a Personal UK Perspective.* Future Healthcare Journal, Vol. 5, No. 3, 2018.

Donker, T., Petrie, K., Proudfoot, J., Clarke, J., Birch, M.R., Christensen, H. *Smartphones for Smarter Delivery of Mental Health Programs: A Systematic Review.* Journal of Medical Internet Research, 2013 Nov 15;15(11):e247.

Doucet, S., Luke, A., Splane, J., Azar, R. *Patient Navigation as an Approach to Improve the Integration of Care: The Case of NaviCare/SoinsNavi.* International Journal of Integrated Care, Vol. 19. No. 4, pg 7, 2019.

Dumasia, L., Harris, E., Drelichman, A. *Quality Performance Improvement with the Implementation of Standard Chemotherapy Order Forms.* Journal of Oncology Practice, Vol. 2. No. 3, 104–107, May 2006.

Elhauge, E. The Fragmentation of U.S. Health Care: Causes and Solutions, 1st Edition, Oxford, 2010.

Enthoven, A.C. *Integrated Delivery Systems: The Cure for Fragmentation.* American Journal of Managed Care, 2009 Dec;15(10 Suppl):S284–90.

Espinoza, J., Shah, P., Raymond, J. *Integrating Continuous Glucose Monitor Data Directly into the Electronic Health Record: Proof of Concept.* Diabetes Technology and Therapeutics, July 2020.

Fanmuy, G. *Lean Systems Engineering Working Group Meeting*, INCOSE 2010 International Symposium, Chicago, July 10–15, 2010.

Flexx, https://www.flexxproductions.com/news/hospital-field-tents-and-medical-testing-tents-from-flexx-productions/, accessed Sept. 11, 2020.

Fuentes, A., Shields, J., Chirumamilla, N., Martinez, M., Kaafarani, H., Yeh, D.D., White, B., Filbin, M., DePesa, C., Velmahos, G., Lee, J. *"One-Way-Street" Streamlined Admission of Critically Ill Trauma Patients Reduces Emergency Department Length of Stay.* Internal and Emergency Medicine, October 2017.

GAO, Space Acquisitions: Major Space Programs Still at Risk for Cost and Schedule Increases, GAO - 08 - 552T, Washington, DC, Mar. 2008b.

Genes, N., Violante, S., Cetrangol, C., Rogers, L., Schadt, E.E., Chan, Y.Y.C. *From Smartphone to EHR: A Case Report on Integrating Patient-Generated Health Data.* Nature. June 2018.

Gladwell, M. The Tipping Point, How Little Things Can make Big Difference, Back Bay Books, 2000.

Goundrey-Smith, S. *Pharmacy Automation.* Information Technology in Pharmacy, 2012.

Graban, M. Lean Hospitals: Improving Quality, Patient Safety, and Employee Engagement, 2nd Edition, CRC Press, 2012.

Granja, C., Almada-Lobo, B., Janela, F., Seabra, J., Mendes, A. *An Optimization based on Simulation Approach to the Patient Admission Scheduling Problem: Diagnostic Imaging Department Case Study.* Journal of Digital Imaging, Vol. 27. No. 1, 33–40, Feb 2014.

Grissinger, M., Litman, R.S. *Pro/Con Debate: Color-Coded Medication Labels – CON: Anesthesia Drugs Should NOT Be Color-Coded.* APSF, Vol. 33. No. 3, February 2019.

Gupta, S., Kapil, S., Sharma, M. *Improvement of Laboratory Turnaround Time using Lean Methodology.* International Journal of Health Care Quality Assurance, Vol. 31. No. 14, 295–308, May 14, 2018.

Hales, B., Terblanche, M., Fowler, R., Sibbald, W. *Development of Medical Checklists for Improved Quality of Patient Care.* International Journal for Quality in Health Care, Vol. 20. No. 1, February 2008.

Harry, M., Schroeder, R. Six Sigma: The Breakthrough Management Strategy Revolutionizing The World's Top Corporations. Currency Doubleday, 2000.

HBR, Ed., *Manufacturing Excellence at Toyota*, Harvard Business School Series, paperback, 2008.

HEALTHNOVEMBER, *Nurse Recruitment: Best Practices for Hiring Top Talent*, https://www.wolterskluwer.com/en/expert-insights/nurse-recruitment-best-practices-for-hiring-top-talent, HEALTHNOVEMBER 06, 2018.

Honour, E. *Systems Engineering Return on Investment*, Paper 11.4.2, INCOSE 2010 International Symposium, Chicago, July 10–15, 2010.

Hovlid, E., Plessen, C.V., Haug, K., Aslaksen, A.B., Bukve, O. *A New Pathway for Elective Surgery to Reduce Cancellation Rates*. BMC Health Services Research, 2012 Jun 11;12:154.

IHI, Closing the Loop: *A Guide to Safer Ambulatory Referrals in the EHR Era*, Cambridge IISE Transactions on Healthcare Systems Engineering (monthly), December 2017.

INCOSE HWG, https://www.incose.org/hwg-past-conferences, last accessed 7–16-2020.

INCOSE, Guide for Writing Requirements Summary Sheet, TechGuideWRsummary2019Soft, INCOSE, 2019.

INCOSE, Systems Engineering Vision 2020, INCOSE-TP-2004-004-02, Rev. 2.03, 2007.

IOM, Crossing the Quality Chasm: A New Health System for the 21st Century, Institute of Medicine, Committee on Quality of Health Care in America, PMID: 25057539, National Academies Press, 2001.

Jacobson, C.T. TRW 1901–2001, TRW Inc., Cleveland, Ohio, 2001.

Jafari, M. *Reducing Turnover Time to Improve Efficiency in the Operating Room*. USF Master's Projects and Capstones, 2017 (note: this reference deals with OR turnover, but some tools and concepts also apply to hospital room turnover).

Jain, K., Sahran, D., Singhal, M., Misra, M.C. *A Novel Way of Linen Management in an Acute Care Surgical Center*. Indian Journal of Surgery, January 2017.

Jimmerson C. Value Stream Mapping for Healthcare Made Easy, ISBN-13: 978-1420078527, Productivity Press, 2010.

Janik, L.S., Vender, J.S. *2020 Pro/Con Debate: Color-Coded Medication Labels – PRO: Color-Coded Medication Labels Improve Patient Safety*. APSF, February 2020.

Kaiser Health News, *Unnecessary Medical Tests, Treatments Cost $200 Billion Annually, Cause Harm*. Kaiser Health News, May 2, 2017.

Kaiser Permanente, https://www.hdrinc.com/portfolio/kaiser-permanente-re-imagining-ambulatory-design, last accessed Sept. 11, 2020.

Kanter, M.H., Lindsay, G., Bellows, J., Chase, A. *Complete Care at Kaiser Permanente: Transforming Chronic and Preventive Care*. The Joint Commission Journal on Quality and Patient Safety, Vol. 39. No. 11, November 2013.

Kappenman, A.M., Ragsdale, R., Rim, M.H., Tyler, L.S., Nickman, N.A. *Implementation of a Centralized Mail-Order Pharmacy Service*. American Journal of Health-system Pharmacy: AJHP: Official Journal of the American Society of Health-system Pharmacists, 2019 Sep 1;76(Supplement_3):S74-S78.

Klas Arch Collaborative Reports on EMRs, https://klasresearch.com/reports, accessed Sept. 11, 2020.

Kohn, L.T., Corrigan, J.M., Donaldson, M.S. To Err is Human: Building a Safer Health System, Institute of Medicine (US) Committee on Quality of Health Care in America, PMID: 25077248, National Academies Press, 2000.

Kurani, N., McDermott, D. *How Does the Quality of the U.S. Healthcare System Compare to Other Countries? KFF Chart Collections.* Quality of Care, July 2020.

Laxmisan, A., Hakimazada, F., Sayan, O.R., Green, R.A., Zhang, J., Patel, V.L. *The Multitasking Clinician: Decision-Making and Cognitive Demand During and After Team Handoffs in Emergency Care.* International Journal of Medical Informatics, 2007;76(11–12):801–11.

Leppin, A.L., Gionfriddo, M.R., Kessler, M., Brito, J.P., Mair, F.S., Gallacher, K., Wang, Z., Erwin, P.J., Sylvester, T., Boehmer, K., Ting, H.T., Murad, M.H., Shippee, N.D., Montori, V.M. *Preventing 30-Day Hospital Readmissions: A Systematic Review and Meta-Analysis of Randomized Trials.* The Journal of the American Medical Association Internal Medicine, July 2014;174(7):1095–1107.

Liker, J. K. The Toyota Way, 14 Management Principles, McGraw Hill, 2004.

Lin, A.C., Jang, R., Sedani, D., Thomas, S., Barker, K.N., Flynn, E.A. *Re-Engineering A Pharmacy Work System and Layout to Facilitate Patient Counseling.* American Journal of Health-System Pharmacy, 1996 53(13):1558–64.

Lippi, G., Chance, J.J., Church, S., et al. *Preanalytical Quality Improvement: From Dream to Reality.* Clinical Chemistry and Laboratory Medicine. 2011.

Lockheed Martin, *Risk and Opportunity Management, webinar,* https://www.lockheedmartin.com/content/dam/lockheed-martin/eo/documents/suppliers/training-2017-risk-opportunity-mgmt.pdf, accessed July 17, 2020.

Lu, P., O'Halloran, A., Williams, W.W., Lindley, M.C., Farrall, S., Bridges, C.B.B. *Racial and Ethnic Disparities in Vaccination Coverage among Adult Population.* American Journal of Preventive Medicine. 2015 Dec;49(6 Suppl 4):S412–25.

McGough, P.M., Jaffy, M.B., Norris, T.E., Sheffield, P., Shumway, M. *Redesigning Your Workspace to Support Team-Based Care.* American Academy of Family Physicians, 2013 Jul-Aug;20(4):6.

Maguire, P. *How to Streamline Discharges. A Medical Center Eliminates Discharge Bottlenecks in the Pharmacy.* Today's Hospitalists, October 2018.

Marcus, C. *Strategies for Improving the Quality of Verbal Patient and Family Education: A Review of the Literature and Creation of the EDUCATE model.* Health Psychology and Behavioral Medicine, 2014 Jan 1;2(1):482–495.

Masland, M.C., Lou, C., Snowden, L. *Use of Communication Technologies to Cost-Effectively Increase the Availability of Interpretation Services in Healthcare Settings.* Telemedicine Journal and E-Health, Jul-Aug 2010;16(6):739–45.

McManus, H.L. Product Development Value Stream Mapping Manual, LAI Release Beta, Massachusetts Institute of Technology, LAI, April 2004.

Morgan, M. J., Liker, J. K. Toyota Product Development System, Productivity Press, 2006.

Murman, E. M., Allen, T., Bozdogan, K., Cutcher – Gershenfeld, J., McManus, H., Nightingale, D., Rebentisch, E., Shields, T., Stahl, F., Walton, M., Warmkessel, J.,

Weiss,. S., Widnall, S. Lean Enterprise Value: Insights from MIT's Lean Aerospace Initiative, Palgrave, Hampshire, 2002.

Ninan, N., Roy, J.C., Thomas, M.R. *Benefits of Cross-Training: Scale Development and Validity.* Prabandhan Indian Journal of Management, Volume 12, Issue 6, June 2019.

Nunn, R. Parsons, J., Shambaugh, J. A Dozen Facts about the Economics of the US Healthcare System, Brookings, March 10, 2020.

Oehmen, J. The Guide to Lean Enablers for Managing Engineering Programs, LAI MIT-PMI-INCOSE, 2012.

Oppenheim, B.W. *Lean Product Development Flow,* J. of Systems Engineering, Vol. 7, No. 4, 2004.

Oppenheim, B.W. Lean for Systems Engineering with Lean Enablers for Systems Engineering, Wiley Series in Systems Engineering and Management, Wiley, 2011.

Oppenheim, B.W., Kanter, M.H., Bueno, O, Dizon, L.D., Farnacio, L.M., Medina, P.L., Moradian, M. M., Tabata, C., Tiffert, M.S. *Lean Enablers for Clinical Laboratories.* Research in Medical & Engineering Sciences, November 27, 2017.

Paine, C.W., Goel, V.V., Ely, E., Stave, C.D., Stemler, S., Zander, M., Bonafide, C.P. *Systematic Review of Physiological Monitor Alarm Characteristics and Pragmatic Interventions to Reduce Alarm Frequency.* Journal of Hospital Medicine, December 2016 Feb;11(2):136–44.

Papalexi, M., Bamford, D., Dehe, B. *A Case Study of Kanban Implementation within the Pharmaceutical Supply Chain.* International Journal of Logistics Research and Applications, Volume 19, 2016 - Issue 4.

Pattin, A.J., *Disparities in the Use of Immunization Services among Underserved Minority Patient Populations and the Role of Pharmacy Technicians: A Review.* Journal of Pharmacy Technology, 2017 Oct; 33(5): 171–176.

Poulter, B., *Ways To Help Eliminate Unscheduled Downtime*, Dassault Systems, February 4, 2015.

Payne, H.E., Lister, C., West, J.H., Bernhardt, J.M. *Behavioral Functionality of Mobile Apps in Health Interventions: A Systematic Review of the Literature.* JMIR Mhealth and Uhealth, Vol 3, No 1 (2015): Jan-Mar.

PCAST, *Better Health Care and Lower Costs: Accelerating Improvement through Systems Engineering*, Report to the President, Presidential Council of Advisors on Science and Technology, White House, 2014.

Pharmacy Technology, https://www.pharmacytechnologysolutions.ca/pharmaclik-rx-doc/Content/Workflow/Workflow%20Tab.htm, accessed Sept. 11, 2020.

Rama, F. D. *Role of a Nurse Navigator and Care Pathways in an Integrated Prostate Cancer Care Program*, Journal of Clinical Pathways, Vol. 5. No. 7. Pg. 33–38, 2019.

Rana, S.V. *No Preanalytical Errors in Laboratory Testing: A Beneficial Aspect for Patients.* Indian Journal of Clinical Biochemistry, 2012 Oct; 27(4): 319–321.

Rebentisch, E. Ed., Integrating Program Management and Systems Engineering: Methods, Tools, and Organizational Systems for Improving Performance, 1st Edition, ISBN-13: 978-1119258926PMI, INCOSE, Wiley, 2017.

Reiling, J., Hughes, R.G., Murphy, M.R. *The Impact of Facility Design on Patient Safety*. Patient Safety and Quality: An Evidenced-Based Handbook for Nurses, Agency for Healthcare Research and Quality (US); April 2008, Chapter 28.

Rivera, A.J., Karsh, B.T. *Interruptions and Distractions in Healthcare: Review and Reappraisal*. Qual Saf Health Care, 2010 August, 19(4): 304–312.

Robinson, E.T., Schafermeyer, K.W. *Cross Training of Hospital Pharmacy Technicians*. Pharmacy Practice Management Quarterly, 1996 Apr;16(1):72–8.

Rodney, H. An Exploration of Healthcare Inventory and Lean Management in Minimizing Medical Supply Waste in Healthcare Organizations, Walden University – ProQuest Dissertations Publishing, 2013.

Safavi, K.C., Driscoll, W., Wiener-Kronish, J.P. *Remote Surveillance Technologies: Realizing the Aim of Right Patient, Right Data, Right Time*. Anesthesia and Analgesia, 2018.

Sinclair, A., Eyre, C., Shuard, R., Correa, J., Guerin, A. *Introduction of Pharmacy Technicians Onto a Busy Oncology Ward as Part of the Nursing Team*. European Journal of Hospital Pharmacy, 2018 Mar; 25(2): 92–95.

Sage, A.P., Rouse, W.B. Handbook of Systems Engineering and Management, 2nd Edition, ISBN-13: 978-0470083536, Wiley, 2020.

Salinas, M., Lopez-Garrigos, M., Flores, E., Gutiérrez, M., Lugo, J., Uris, J. *Three Years of Preanalytical Errors: Quality Specifications and Improvement through Implementation of Statistical Process Control*. Scandinavian Journal of Clinical and Laboratory Investigation. 2009;69(8):822-6.

Sendelbach, S., Funk, M. *Alarm Fatigue: A Patient Safety Concern*. Advanced Critical Care, Oct-Dec 2013;24(4):378–86.

Serper, M., Volk, M.L. *Current and Future Applications of Telemedicine Optimize the Delivery of Care in Chronic Liver Disease*. Clin Gastroenterol Hepatol. 2018 Feb; 16(2): 157–161.

Smith, C.D., Balatbat, C., Corbridge, S., Dopp, A.L., Fried, J., Harter, R., Landefeld, S., Martin, C.Y., Opelka, F., Sandy, L., Sato, L., Sinsky, C. *Implementing Optimal Team-Based Care to Reduce Clinician Burnout*. National Academy of Medicine, September 2018.

Solet, J.M., Barach, P.R. *Managing Alarm Fatigue in Cardiac Care*. Progress in Pediatric Cardiology, January 2012, 33(1):85–90.

Speicher, S., https://sean-story.wistia.com/medias/bs62oygize, accessed Sept. 11, 2020.

Spewak, S.H., Zachman, J.A., Hill, S.C. Enterprise Architecture Planning: Developing a Blueprint for Data, Applications, and Technology, Wiley, 1992.

Sullivan, P., Soefje, S., Reinhart, D., McGeary, C., Cabie, E.D. *Using Lean Methodology to Improve Productivity in a Hospital Oncology Pharmacy*. American Journal of Health-System Pharmacy, 2014 Sep 1;71(17):1491–8.

The UK Royal Academy of Engineering, *Engineering Better Care*, 2017.

Verbano, C., Crema, M., Nicosia, F. *Visual Management System to Improve Care Planning and Controlling: The Case of Intensive Care Unit*. Production Planning and Control – The Management of Operations, June 2017.

Walden, D.D., Roedler, G.J., Forsberg, K.J., Hamelin, R. D., Shortell, T.M. Systems Engineering Handbook: A Guide for System Life Cycle Processes and Activities, 4th Edition, INCOSE, ISBN: 978-1-118-99940-0, 2015.

Wang, B.N., Brummond, P., Stevenson, J.G. *Comparison of Barcode Scanning by Pharmacy Technicians and Pharmacists' Visual Checks for Final Product Verification.* American Journal of Health-System Pharmacy. 2016 Mar 1;73(5):266.

Ward, B. *Close the Loop on Test Results.* Patient Safety Monitor Journal, February 18, 2020.

Wedgewood, I. Lean Six Sigma, A Practitioner's Guide, Prentice Hall, 2007.

Vernon, D., Brown, J.E., Griffiths, E., Nevill, A.M., Pinkney, M. *Reducing Readmission Rates through a Discharge Follow-Up Service.* Future Healthcare Journal, 2019 Jun;6(2):114–117. (This text is for hospitals, but also applies to clinics).

Wikipedia, "V-Model", Accessed July 2, 2020.

Womack, J.P., Jones, D.T. Lean Thinking. Simon & Shuster, 1996.

Womack, J.P., Jones, D.T., Roos, D. The Machine That Changed the World, The Story of Lean Production, The MIT International Motor Vehicle Program, Harper – Perennial, 1990.

Yoshida, H., Rutman, L.E., Chen, J., Enriquez, B.K., Woodward, G.A., Mazor, S.S., *Waterfalls and Handoffs: A Novel Physician Staffing Model to Decrease Handoffs in a Pediatric Emergency Department.* Annals of Emergency Medicine – An International Journal, 2019 Mar;73(3):248–254.

Zubatsky, M., Pettinelli, D., Salas, J., Davis, D. *Associations Between Integrated Care Practice and Burnout Factors of Primary Care Physicians.* Family Medicine, 2018; 50(10):770-774.

Glossary of Abbreviations

A1C: A blood test measuring a 3-month average level of blood glucose

AoA: Analysis of Alternatives

AMA: American Medical Association

ASEE: American Society of Electrical Engineers

ASME: American Society of Mechanical Engineers

AYA: Adolescents and Young Adults – a distinct group of cancer patients

CaPA: California Physicians Alliance

CDC: Center for Disease Control

ConOps or CONOPS: Concept of Operations

COVID-19: Coronavirus causing the 2020 pandemic

CS VSM: Current State Value Stream Map, a tool of Lean

DF1: Data Flow View 1 (one of DODAF views)

DME: Durable Medical Equipment

DODAF: Department of Defense Architectural Framework

Dx: Diagnosis

ED: Emergency Department

EHR: Electronic Health Record

EKG: Electrocardiogram

EVS: Environmental Services

FS VSM: Future State Value Stream Map, a tool of Lean

GDP: Gross Domestic Product

HSE: Healthcare Systems Engineering

IAE: Institution for the Advancement of Engineering

ICU: Intensive Care Unit

INCOSE: International Council on Systems Engineering, professional society of Systems Engineers

IOM: Institute of Medicine

ISOPE: International Society of Petroleum Engineers

IT: Information Technology
LA: Los Angeles
LAI: Lean Advancement Initiative
LAI EdNet: Educational Network of Universities under LAI
LEfSE: Lean Enablers for Systems Engineering
LH: Lean Healthcare
LHSE: Lean Healthcare Systems Engineering
MBSE: Model Based Systems Engineering
MD: Medical Doctor
MEiL: [Wydział] Mechaniczny Energetyki i Lotnictwa (name of a Department in Warsaw Institute of Technology)
MIT: Massachusetts Institute of Technology
MoE: Measures of Effectiveness
NASA: National Aeronautics and Astronautics Agency
NIH: National Institute of Health
NPAJAC: National Polish American Jewish American Council
OECD: Organization for Economic Cooperation and Development
OR: Operating Room
OV1: Operational View 1 (one of DODAF views)
PCAST: Presidential Council of Advisors on Science and Technology
PCP: Primary Care Provider
POGO: name of longitudinal oscillations of liquid rockets
RN: Registered Nurse
SE: Systems Engineering
SIPOC: Source-Input-Process-Output-Customer diagram
SNAME: Society of Naval Architects and Marine Engineers
SNF: Skilled Nursing Facility
SV1: Systems View 1 (one of DODAF views)
TQM: Total Quality Management
TRW: An Aerospace company named after Thompson, Ramo, and Wooldridge
Tx: Treatment
UCLA: University of California, Los Angeles
UK: United Kingdom
USC Keck/LA: University of Southern California Keck and Los Angeles County Medical Center
VA: Veterans Administration medical center
V&V: Verification and Validation
VSM: Value Stream Map (or Mapping)
WHO: World Health Organization

Appendix

Chapter 2 of this book described the new Lean Healthcare Systems Engineering (LHSE) process. For completeness, two other systems engineering processes are mentioned in this Appendix:

1. The UK Royal Academy of Engineering, Medical Sciences Systems Engineering Model titled "Engineering Better Care" [Royal Academy, 2017]. It is an elegant approach for the design of complex medical and healthcare systems. In the opinion of the present author, it is suitable for much larger systems than those discussed in this book and described by the LHSE process. The model is illustrated in Fig. A-1.

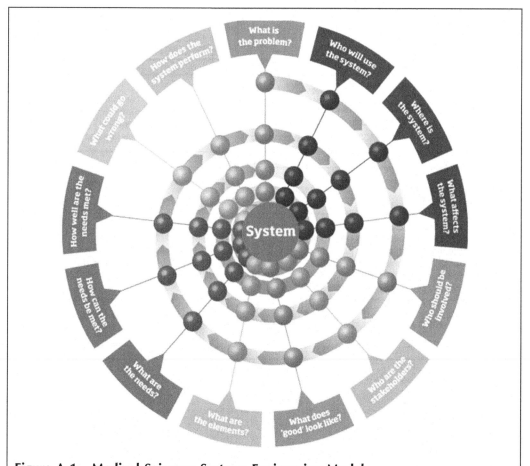

Figure A-1 Medical Sciences Systems Engineering Model.

[The UK Royal Academy of Engineering, 2017, by permission]

2. The ISO 15288 Systems Engineering life-cycle processes are illustrated in Fig. A-2, after [Walden, 2015]. This sequence of processes is intended for large complex technology programs and matches the federal acquisition system. Again, these processes would be overkill for small healthcare delivery projects. The reader will notice that only a few of the processes shown have been included in LHSE: Design, Architecture, Risk, Implementation. Verification, Validation, and Operation[alization], and these have been implemented in LHSE in a dramatically simpler way

Technical processes
* Business or mission analysis process
* Stakeholder needs & requirements definition process
* System requirements definition process
* Architecture definition process
* Design definition process
* System analysis process
* Implementation process
* Integration process
* Verification process
* Transition process
* Validation process
* Operation process
* Maintenance process
* Disposal process

Technical management processes
* Project planning process
* Project assessment and control process
* Decision management process
* Risk management process
* Configuration management process
* Information management process
* Measurement process
* Quality assurance process

Agreement processes
* Acquisition process
* Supply process

Organizational project-enabling processes
* Life cycle model management process
* Infrastructure management process
* Portfolio management process
* Human resource management process
* Quality management process
* Knowledge management process

Figure A-2   ISO 15288 Systems Engineering Processes.

Author's Biography

Bohdan "Bo" W. Oppenheim was born in Warsaw, Poland. His professional background includes healthcare, engineering, systems engineering, and Lean. He has lived in the United States since 1971. His degrees include a PhD (1980) from the University of Southampton, U.K.; a Naval Architect's postgraduate degree (1974) from MIT; an M.S. (1972) from Stevens Institute of Technology in New Jersey; and a B.S. (equivalent, 1970), from the Warsaw Technical University, Mechanical Engineering and Aeronautics ("MEiL").

Dr. Oppenheim has worked at Loyola Marymount University, Los Angeles since 1982, and he has held various titles including Professor, Director and creator of Healthcare Systems Engineering 2013–present; Professor of Systems Engineering 2004–present; and Professor and Graduate Director of Mechanical Engineering 1995–2009. Other notable roles include Founder and Co-Chair of Lean Systems Engineering Working Group of INCOSE and leader of the Prototype team developing Lean Enablers for Systems Engineering (LEfSE) (awarded INCOSE Best Product Award, and Shingo Award in 2010); Director of the U.S. Department of Energy Industrial Assessment Center (assessed 125 industrial plants for Lean productivity, 2000–2007); Member of INCOSE Healthcare Working Group; Coordinator of MIT-based Lean Advancement Initiative Educational Network (LAI EdNet); Member of the Steering Committee of the Lean Education Academic Network.

His areas of specialization include Healthcare Systems Engineering, Lean Healthcare Systems Engineering (LHSE) process, Lean Healthcare, productivity, quality, resiliency, systems engineering, and formerly: dynamics, signal processing, vessel mooring simulators, and naval architecture. He is the author (with S. Rubin) of the POGO oscillation simulator for liquid rockets, used by the rocket industry and NASA, and developed at The Aerospace Corporation. His industrial experience (full or part time) includes Aerospace Corporation (1990–1994), Northrop (1985–1990), Global Marine Development (1974–1978). He was a consultant to Northrop–Grumman (2007–2008), Boeing (2001–2004), Airbus (2005), Telekomunikacja Polska (2006–2008), Mars (2007–2008), and 50 other firms and governmental institutions in the U.S. and Europe. He is a member of International Council on Systems Engineering, (INCOSE), LAI EdNet, and formerly American Society of Electrical Engineers (ASEE), American Society of Mechanical Engineers (ASME), ISOPE, and SNAME. Some of his awards and recognitions include three Shingo Awards; Fulbright Award, 2011; Fellow, INCOSE and IAE; Awarded Best Engineering Teacher by the Los

Angeles Council of Engineers and Scientists, 2008. He has been awarded $1,922,000 in externally funded grants.

Dr. Oppenheim is the author of four professional books, 6 professional book chapters, 36 technical journal articles, as well as three non-technical books, 12 articles, and he produced and directed two TV programs. He has presented 20 workshops, tutorials, and webinars on Healthcare Systems Engineering; another 25 on Lean Enablers for Systems Engineering; and 13 workshops, tutorials, and webinars on Lean Product Development Flow. He has been a guest lecturer in Canada, China, France, Germany, Israel, Italy, Netherlands, Poland, Russia, Sweden, the United Kingdom, and the United States.

Dr. Oppenheim lives in Santa Monica, California, and Warsaw, Poland. He has two married sons. He has a U.S. Coast Guard Captain license and is an ocean sailor with 15000 mile experience. He is also a collector of modern Polish art. Web page: https://cse.lmu.edu/media/lmucse/departments/healthcaresystemsengineering/Oppenheim-CV-Feb-2020_V3.pdf.

Index